THE FAR SIDE OF CONSCIOUSNESS

ALSO BY DANIEL COHEN

Voodoo, Devils, and the New Invisible World
Masters of the Occult
A Modern Look at Monsters
Mysterious Places
Myths of the Space Age

FOR YOUNGER READERS

The Magic Art of Foreseeing the Future
In Search of Ghosts
Talking with Animals
The Age of Giant Mammals
Secrets from Ancient Graves

THE FAR SIDE OF CONSCIOUSNESS

Daniel Cohen

ILLUSTRATED

DODD, MEAD & COMPANY · NEW YORK

Copyright © 1974 by Daniel Cohen
All rights reserved
No part of this book may be reproduced in any form
without permission in writing from the publisher

ISBN: 0-396-07002-7
Library of Congress Catalog Card Number: 74-11797
Printed in the United States of America
by The Haddon Craftsmen, Scranton, Penna.

To Carol and Richard Jones

CONTENTS

1. Captain Mitchell's Conversion 1
2. Mind Meditation and Machine 10
3. Doing the Impossible 40
4. Faith Healing 53
5. Extrasensory Dreaming 87
6. Exotic Psychic Phenomena 117
7. Altered States of Consciousness 137
8. Human Programming 156
9. The Science of Religious Experience 183
Selected Bibliography 207
Index 210

ILLUSTRATIONS

Following page 118

Captain Edgar D. Mitchell before the Apollo 14 flight.
Captain Edgar D. Mitchell discusses the results of his unofficial ESP test from space.
Drawing of a European fakir with his trick swords and arrows.
A Hindu holy man displays his indifference to pain.
Levitation is another ability commonly claimed by holy men.
Healing by the laying on of hands.
An experiment in dream telepathy.
The agent tries to transmit the target picture to the sleeping subject.
Dr. Stanley Krippner asks the subject to record her recollections on tape.
The subject picks the painting that corresponds to her dreams.
Significant sections from a dream report.

ILLUSTRATIONS

The target picture in a precognitive dream experiment.
Early hypnotism or magnetism was a favorite subject for cartoonists.
A parlor demonstration of hypnotism.
In *The Cabinet of Dr. Caligari* the hypnotist exercised absolute control over his zombie-like subject.
The astral body departing after death.
The astral body connected to the physical body.
The striking effects of Kirlian photography.
The Children of God during one of their dramatic demonstrations.
A young man speaking in tongues.
Sir Alister Hardy.

1
CAPTAIN MITCHELL'S CONVERSION

ALL through the 1960s the image of the United States astronauts was carefully nurtured by the National Aeronautics and Space Administration's huge public relations operation. The astronauts were clean-cut and clean-living; well-balanced and intelligent, though not overly intellectual; they were practical, hardheaded fellows, certainly not the kind given to entertaining strange or unorthodox ideas.

The astronauts weren't really that standardized, of course. Nobody is that standardized. It was all a painfully constructed public relations screen. These men were groomed to be national heroes, and as such there was a deliberate attempt to show them as men without any faults. The American public was, after all, paying enormous sums of money to put them on the moon, a technological feat for which there was no immediate practical benefit. Apparently it was felt that if any of these expensive heroes turned out to have feet of clay, the public might become restive. One astronaut who had marital difficulties was washed out of the program.

What the NASA public relations folk had failed to take

into account, however, is that people without faults or quirks are extremely uninteresting. Christopher Columbus (to whom the astronauts were continually being compared in those days) was a monumental egotist, and something of a charlatan. He was also a very interesting individual.

The first moon landing on July 20, 1969, was the high point of the entire space program. After that it was all downhill as boredom and eventually real resentment against the high cost of sending men to the moon set in. When the U.S. manned space program ended for all practical purposes early in 1974, there were few public expressions of grief, except from those actually employed by NASA. The passing of the Apollo program had all the public impact of the dropping of a pin.

I spent the night of the first moon landing in a New York radio studio as part of a panel whose purpose it was to fill in the dead spots of the coverage of the landing with what we all hoped was lively and intelligent commentary. That evening one of the other panelists (a cynical fellow, without doubt) predicted that within four years half of the people in America would no longer remember the names of the first two Americans to have stepped on the moon.

At that moment of high excitement, such a prediction seemed rash and foolish. After all, doesn't everybody remember Columbus, and that was nearly five hundred years ago. In mid-1973 I decided to test this "rash" prediction by conducting an informal survey of my own. Out of seventy-five people questioned, only three remembered both names, while another seven could name only the first man. (In case you have forgotten, the first man to step on the moon was Neil Armstrong, the second, Edwin "Buzz" Aldrin.) My cynical colleague, it seems, had been too optimistic.

Perhaps if NASA public relations had not turned out quite

CAPTAIN MITCHELL'S CONVERSION

such a homogenized product, we might at least be able to remember the names of the astronauts.

If the names of the astronauts are largely forgotten, then memory of what they were supposed to do on the moon (aside from picking up a few moon rocks and planting a flag) has faded even faster. Indeed most of the scientific program was never of any interest to the average United States citizen, few understood it or made any attempt to. Out of the large series of complicated, important, but unremembered experiments only one stood out as being genuinely unusual, and thus genuinely memorable.

Captain Edgar D. Mitchell, one of the three astronauts of Apollo 14, conducted a wholly unorthodox and wholly unofficial experiment that probably attracted more attention than any other experiment in the program. It concerned extrasensory perception. Mitchell tried to project the five standard ESP symbols—a star, cross, circle, wavy lines and square, in a particular order, to a preselected percipient on earth. It was the first extrasensory perception experiment conducted from space (though there have been persistent, and persistently unconfirmed, rumors that the Russians had also been conducting space-oriented ESP tests). The success of Mitchell's experiment is open to question, and Mitchell himself considers it only "reasonably successful," though he claims that the odds against the results he obtained occurring by pure chance are 3,000 to one.

After returning to earth, Astronaut Mitchell did something even more unusual. He retired from the space program and from the navy, in which he had been a career officer, and went full time into the psychic field. Over the last few years he has become an enthusiastic evangelist for the psychic. He lectures, appears regularly on television and radio talk shows, and has become the most influential advocate for psychical research in the world today. He is also very probably the astronaut whose name will be best remembered by the majority of the American public. Captain Mitchell has even abandoned the astronaut's traditional clean-cut look and grown a beard.

Captain Mitchell's conversion to the psychic is symbolic. Over the last ten years interest in what has been called psychic phenomena has grown enormously. Today over 100 colleges and universities in the United States are offering courses in various psychic subjects.

This sudden proliferation of psychic courses is due more to pressure from below—that is, to interest from students—than to any new scientific respectability for the subject. The space program, in contrast, never really caught the public fancy for long, despite millions spent on publicity.

Enthusiasts for the psychic insist that they are truly engaged in a scientific search, and that their subject is very definitely becoming more scientifically respectable. They are fond of quoting the results of a poll conducted among the readers of *New Scientist,* a respected British scientific publication whose readership is made up primarily of scientists and technicians. According to the poll, 70 percent of *New Scientist*'s readers at least believed in the possibility of extrasensory perception.

The enthusiasts also remind the skeptics that in 1969 the American Association for the Advancement of Science (AAAS), America's most prestigious and "legitimate" scientific body, the very citadel of the "scientific Establishment" finally admitted to membership the Parapsychological Association, a body of professional workers in the field. The parapsychologists' application had been turned down flat on three previous occasions. This time, though, it received strong support from the eminent anthropologist, Margaret

Mead. Said Professor Mead, "The whole history of scientific advance is full of scientists investigating phenomena that the Establishment did not believe were there." The application was approved by a whopping majority. Professor Mead has since become president of the AAAS.

But if the investigation itself has become more respectable, that does not automatically mean that the parapsychologists are measurably closer to proving that the phenomena they investigate really exist. Though many say that the proof is already there if one would only trouble to read the results of nearly one hundred years of investigation, this contention is highly debatable. Many who have followed the investigation claim that the proof is not there, and that what ESP really stands for is "error some place."

Another major problem concerns the scope of the investigation. Terms like psychic or psi, paranormal or supranormal (the word supernatural is frowned upon) are tossed around quite freely. Yet there is no general agreement as to what they mean. Traditionally psychical research concerned itself with such things as measuring people's alleged telepathic abilities, or investigating haunted houses and reports of poltergeists. But in the 1970s the scope of psychical research or parapsychology has expanded considerably, and its borders have become more blurred than ever. Some of the investigations may more properly lie in the realm of orthodox psychology or even biology.

Into the jungle of terminology and jargon that already infests the field Captain Mitchell has introduced a new term, noetics, the study of consciousness. Though one might think that the last thing psychical research really needed was another Greek word, noetics is an exceptionally useful one, because it is broad enough to take in a whole range of related subjects.

Writing in *The New York Times* about his growing involvement in the field, Captain Mitchell also provides an excellent insight into just what is so compelling about this search:

"My interest in psychic research had actually begun as a search for concepts that would explain and give meaning to life—concepts that I had not found during 25 years of searching in religion and philosophy. The more I got into it, however, the more it became clear that the evidence of psychic research was taking me right back to where I had started. But this time it was on a basis that appeared to offer rational and substantial support for many theological and philosophical concepts and an explanation of why people throughout history had persisted in claiming a spiritual foundation to the physical world.

"To be brief, the evidence of psychic research suggests that awareness can operate externally to the body and that therefore it is not unreasonable to hypothesize that mind may be able to operate independently of the body. . . . psychic research has already put us in a position where it appears that science's basic concept of man and universe must be revised to some degree."

Mitchell's broad view is not an entirely new one. F. W. Myers, one of the founders of psychical research, said nearly three quarters of a century ago that the most important question that could be answered by psychical research is, "Is the Universe friendly?" J. B. Rhine, the grand old man of American parapsychology, who first popularized the card guessing tests in the 1930s, always insisted that he was not really interested in just finding out whether some people were better at guessing cards than others, but rather what is the basic nature of man. The late Bishop James A. Pike spoke of psychical research as exploring areas, "which have to do with the extension of human consciousness beyond the space-time continuum." Pike added his belief that psychical research could provide the sort of information upon which one could build a rational and empirical basis for a belief in the survival of the human personality after death.

The questions are, as you can see, big ones, and the whole problem rests squarely on the concept of consciousness. Is the universe as perceived through our normal senses under ordinary conditions the real and only universe? Is reality only that which can be measured, photographed or embalmed? Are the perceptions of psychics, mystics and seers also valid perceptions of reality? Are there "other realities" which most of us fail to experience or experience only for fleeting instants? Most of us have experienced a strange "hunch" which came true, or a sense of *déjà vu,* and a surprisingly large percentage of us have had far more striking experiences which might be classified as paranormal or even mystic.

The investigator of the psychic, however, faces a paradoxical and perhaps impossible task. He is trying to observe, through normal sensory means, phenomena that are said to be beyond the normal reach of our senses. He also tries to explain them through rational and logical exposition, though centuries of mystics have firmly declared that such phenomena are beyond the reach of human intelligence and cannot be described, only experienced.

Arthur Koestler, a well-known writer, discussed the implications of parapsychology in his book *The Roots of Coincidence.* He concluded, "The limitations of our biological equipment may condemn us to the role of Peeping Toms at the keyhole of eternity. But at least let us take the stuffing out of the keyhole, which blocks even our limited view."

In this book we are going to look at some of the more

recent attempts to get the stuffing out of the Koestlerian keyhole, to overcome, or at least to understand, our own biological limitations. The examination covers a broad range, from the power that our minds have over our own bodies to the powers that some claim to have over the bodies and minds of others for good or ill. We will discuss dreams, out of the body trips, human programming, and attempts that are now being made to develop a science of religious experience.

All of these subjects concern the frontiers, or fringes, if one wishes to be less polite, of the study of human consciousness. The subjects vary in respectability in the eyes of the orthodox. Study of mind-body interaction is quite respectable, though many would disagree with some of the far-flung conclusions that have been made on the basis of such studies. A science of religious experience, however, is only marginally respectable. I have tried to concentrate on serious attempts to explore these subjects, no matter how unorthodox or bizarre these attempts might look and sound. Professional psychics who tour the world making stage and television appearances claiming that "psychic forces" are responsible for what are clearly sleight of hand, are not serious. They are humbugs, and we shall try to ignore them. "Psychic surgeons" who claim to be able to make incisions and remove diseased organs by "psychic" means alone are not only humbugs, they are dangerous. In the pursuit of truth, error is inevitable, so is disagreement, but this does not mean we must tolerate any form of nonsense, just so that we can claim we are being "open-minded." That demeans the subject, and I'm not going to make easy points by taking potshots at obvious frauds and crackpots.

When I first began investigating these subjects nearly a decade ago, I was a skeptic and a materialist. Someone accused me of having an eighteenth-century mind, and I took that as a compliment. I remain both a skeptic and a materialist today. Yet, over the years I have developed a grudging respect for the persistence and ingenuity of the explorers of the psychic world. The subject commands the devoted attention of too many millions either to be left entirely in the hands of the professional praise singers or to be ignored as unworthy. So it is with a generous measure of skepticism, tempered by respect and a compelling interest, that I offer this look at the far side of consciousness.

2
MIND MEDITATION AND MACHINE

IN Los Angeles there is (or was) an organization called The Church of the Sacred Alpha, while San Diego was the home of the Holy Feedback Church. These two "churches" and similar institutions throughout the world are far out, but probably inevitable developments from the current fascination with two concepts: biofeedback and brain waves, and the closely allied interest in meditation.

Biofeedback is a general term for a whole variety of techniques by which an individual is made aware of certain internal states or functions of which he would otherwise be unaware. A very simple form of biofeedback would be listening to one's heartbeat with a stethoscope. Another of these internal states is brain activity. Not thought, mind you; we are not consciously aware of the electrical activity within our brain which may (or may not) be the basis of what we call thought.

For a long time it has been known that the cells of the living brain generate weak electrical charges. Pioneering work on measuring these charges was done in the late 1920s by the German scientist Hans Berger who developed the electroencephalograph or EEG. By painlessly attaching electrodes to a subject's scalp Berger was able to record electrical activity taking place within the brain. His first machine was attached to an oscilloscope which transformed the electrical potentials within the brain into a visual signal. The signal was seen as a wavy line and the electrical activity of the brain was given the name "brain waves." These brain waves are the total measure of the electrical activity of a large number of individual cells. This electrical activity is extremely weak and must be greatly amplified in order to be recorded by the EEG. Later the machine was adapted to use a moving pen and an unwinding sheet of graph paper so that there could be a permanent record of the brain waves.

Berger had some interesting theories about the brain activity that his EEG was measuring. He even believed that he might be able to measure the energy responsible for extrasensory perception. But this work was not appreciated by the increasingly powerful Nazi party. As the Nazis began to take control of academic life in Germany, Berger was forced to resign his university post. He committed suicide a few years later. For a long time the EEG remained little more than an interesting scientific oddity.

The tracings of the EEG machine give no hint of what a person is thinking, but they do seem, in a very general sort of way, to indicate certain broad psychological states. The brain wave pattern of a person who is awake and alert looks quite different than the pattern recorded from the same person while asleep. Diagnostically the EEG has been most useful in recognizing epilepsy. Just before and during a seizure the epileptic's brain produces a very particular kind of brain wave pattern. Persons with suspected brain injuries are often given EEG tests in an attempt to pinpoint the injury. The normally functioning brain produces a number of characteristic patterns. There are four recognized classes of brain waves, all tagged with Greek letters: alpha, beta, delta and theta.

The slowest are the delta, which register up to four cycles per second. These are the waves most prominent in the EEG of a subject who is sleeping deeply, but not dreaming. Dreamers' brains generate more theta waves, from four to eight cycles per second. Theta waves have also been related to drowsiness and oddly to moments of creativity. The fastest of the waves are the beta, registering from thirteen to twenty-six cycles per second, and even faster in certain cases of mental illness. Among the general run of the population the beta waves are associated with periods of concentration and anxiety. But the brain waves that have received the most attention recently are the alpha, which run from eight to thirteen cycles per second and are associated with a state that has often been described as "relaxed awareness."

The picture presented by the tracings of the EEG machine, however, is far from simple. The brain, particularly the awake brain, may show a variety of tracings—alpha, beta, theta—at any given time. Moreover, different parts of the brain can produce different types of tracings. The right hemisphere of the brain can be generating alpha waves, while the left is generating beta. The next moment this may be reversed. Not all alpha waves, or any of the other waves, are the same in all individuals or at all times. Some waves are stronger, that is, of greater amplitude than others.

Psychologists also realize that the readings obtained by taping electrodes to the outside of the skull are weak and woefully incomplete. It is a bit like trying to discover what lives in the sea by examining only what floats to the surface. A far better picture of the brain's electrical activity could be obtained by planting electrodes directly inside the brain, though it is obvious why there would be few volunteers for such experiments. Still, inadequate and puzzling as they are, the EEG readings of brain activity are just about the only game in town. They provide an objective measure of activity within the living brain and they have proved useful in certain lines of research.

In the late 1950s and early 1960s there was a great deal of laboratory research carried out on sleep and dreams. Here the EEG proved a valuable tool. The research confirmed what most people had suspected anyway—that there were several different "stages" or levels of sleep. During each of these stages the EEG registers markedly different patterns of brain activity.

Another discovery coming out of this sleep research was that dreams, rather than being occasional and infrequent occurrences, are part of the normal sleep cycle for every one of us. While certain EEG readings were typical of dream states, the best way of finding out whether a sleeper was dreaming was to find out what his eyes were doing. Electrodes pasted near the eyes were able to detect movement beneath the closed lids. When the readings showed that the sleeper's eyes were moving rapidly, that was a sign that he was dreaming. It was almost as though the sleeper's eyes were trying to follow the action of his dream beneath his closed lids.

Shortly before a subject fell asleep his brain usually recorded a well-defined pattern of brain waves in which alpha dominated. Alpha activity occurs at other times, generally when a subject is sitting with closed eyes in a relaxed and comfortable position and not thinking about much of anything.

For Dr. Joe Kamiya, one of those who was doing research on sleep at the University of Chicago, this raised two interesting questions. First, did people whose brains were registering strong alpha rhythms know that there was something different about the way in which their brain was operating at that moment than at other moments? Secondly, if they did know, would it be possible to control this brain activity? Still another reason for investigating the alpha state particularly is that the pattern is usually very clear, and thus it is relatively easy to investigate.

In his initial experiment Kamiya put his wired-up subject into a darkened room and periodically asked him whether or not he was generating alpha rhythms. Kamiya could check the subject's answers against the EEG tracings on the graph paper. The subject guessed right about 50 percent of the time, sheer chance, and a good indication that he had no idea what his brain was doing. But as the experiment proceeded, a fascinating thing began to happen. The subject was informed whether he guessed right or wrong each time, and this apparently made him more aware of the alpha state. After four days of tests he was able to guess correctly when he was in an alpha or non-alpha every single time.

If the alpha state could be recognized, could it also be controlled? The answer proved to be yes. After a relatively short period Kamiya found that most subjects were able to "turn on" alpha states almost at will. In order to facilitate this training, Kamiya devised a labor-saving biofeedback system. Instead of having someone sitting at an EEG console telling the subject when he was in an alpha state, Kamiya's device sounded a tone whenever alpha waves were registered by the EEG. The object of training was to keep the tone on as long as possible.

Some subjects can produce alpha with ease while others find the task maddening. Those who try hard to keep the tone on merely succeed in tensing up and shutting the tone off. Making an effort to relax and slip into the alpha state is a bit like following the command "try not to think of a blue monkey." The harder you try not to, the more you do. The secret seems to be simply to let the mind drift, but for many that isn't easy.

Actually there are a number of ways in which a person can produce the alpha rhythm without relaxing, thinking of nothing or shutting his eyes. One way is to roll your eyes up as far as you can. Another way is to focus and defocus on a distant object. In fact, switching alpha on and off is so easy that it was once considered as a possible means of communication. Dr. Edmund Dewan of the U.S. Air Force attached subjects who were trained to control alpha to a device which switched on a light every time alpha registered on an EEG. The hope was that astronauts might somehow be able to use similar equipment as an emergency means of communication. The subjects were able to switch the light on and off in Morse code fashion, but as a means of communication this method proved to be exceptionally slow and cumbersome, and further work with the system was abandoned.

But eyeball rolling and focusing and defocusing to produce alpha are in a sense cheating. Kamiya's work was concerned not only with a reading on an EEG machine, but with what the reading reflected about the subject's internal mental state. He improved his original device in order to relay the intensity of the brain wave patterns, the greater the amplitude—the lower the tone. Different tones were used to signify wave patterns other than alpha. Experiments have shown that people can learn to recognize and to a certain extent control beta, theta and even delta states. But popular interest has remained focused on the alpha state. Why? The answer may have more to do with the state of our society than with any advances in the study of brain activity.

There is nothing particularly supercharged or ecstatic or

even unusual about the alpha state. You can probably put yourself into alpha very simply and quickly. Get comfortable, relax, close your eyes and think of nothing in particular. After a short while you may fall asleep or get jumpy and move about, but before that happens you have probably been generating alpha waves. Not exactly a life-changing experience, you will agree.

Besides, everybody does not experience the alpha state in the same way. Most of those who have been tested find the alpha state pleasant and relaxing. A few find it exciting, while a few others report feelings of anxiety and fear. As I said, since no one really knows what brain wave patterns mean, there is no way of making absolute correlations between the readings and subjective states of feeling.

A good part of what one experiences in alpha appears to depend upon what one expects to experience. In one test a subject reported time and space distortions while in the alpha state. A short while later, though, while the subject was still generating strong alpha waves, the experimenter told him that the alpha waves had ceased. The subject then reported that the time and space distortions also vanished.

The results of Kamiya's research began to creep into the popular press in the late 1960s. It was a time when there was an increasing interest among a significant portion of the population, especially students and other young people, in what was happening inside themselves, particularly inside of their own heads. This interest began with the widespread popularity of a variety of psychoactive drugs like LSD. There was a great deal of talk of "exploring inner space" and discovering "new realities," and there was the strongly held belief that the drug experience could alter one's entire way of life, in addition to providing a pleasant and exciting high.

It wasn't long before a reaction against drug use had set

in. Many of the users had unpleasant, even horrifying experiences. The nondrug-using majority of society, including the governmental and legal authorities, responded with violent revulsion. Not only was the casual use of LSD made illegal, but the government banned almost all legitimate research with the substance.

The bloom was off the drug scene, but the interest in inner trips persisted. The "alpha trip" became one of them. Student volunteers displayed an enthusiasm for participating in alpha feedback experiments that far exceeded normal interest in psychological experiments. Eric Peper, a New York University psychologist, recalls being awakened at two in the morning by a telephone call from a student in California who wanted to become an alpha research subject. Peper also noted that one could see students wandering around the N.Y.U. campus wearing headsets with earphones—trying to get a tone signifying alpha.

The fascination with inner realities almost inevitably led to another peak in the Western world's off-and-on fascination with Eastern philosophy and religion and with the practice of meditation. Typical, perhaps, was the experience of the singing group the Beatles, youth culture heroes of the early 1960s. After considerable experience with LSD, the group fell under the influence of the Maharishi Mahesh Yogi, an ascetic-looking Indian guru who taught a technique called transcendental meditation. Transcendental meditation was supposed to be a quick and painless method of attaining serenity and self-awareness without the use of drugs, violent exercises, or any drastic alternations in ordinary lifestyles. The Maharishi was only one of a score of gurus or masters who had attracted the attention of wealthy Westerners.

Along with this new interest in Eastern philosophy and religion, there was also considerable skepticism that the Indian yogis, or their Japanese counterparts, the Zen masters, had anything to teach the West, or that they had anything at all. Experiments with physical monitoring devices had shown that the yogis possessed remarkable physical control, but physical control is only part of yoga. Indeed the physical side of yoga or Hatha yoga is considered inferior to the practice of the meditative yoga or Raja yoga.

We Westerners have a passion for objective measurement. We wanted to find out if the meditating yogi really was in a different state of consciousness, or just relaxing with his eyes closed. After considerable difficulty, Marion A. Wenger of UCLA and Basu K. Bagchi of the University of Michigan Medical School managed to enlist the cooperation of fourteen of these holy men. They were fitted up with the usual electrodes, then sat down in the lotus position, closed their eyes and began to meditate. The EEG recorded strong alpha rhythms, often continuing for several hours.

The yogis did not fall asleep or grow restless; on the contrary, they remained extremely relaxed, but wide awake. One measure of relaxation is the electrical resistance of the skin; the lower the resistance, the higher the anxiety; the higher the resistance, the greater the relaxation. The conductivity of the skin is influenced by moisture, water being a good conductor of electricity. Anxiety brings on sweating and thus lowers the resistance of the skin to a tiny electrical charge. Sweaty palms is a well-known sign of anxiety. The electrical resistance of the skin is one of the three measurements made by the polygraph or lie detector. In all the meditating yogis the electrical resistance of their skin rose sharply over that shown by the same subjects when they were just sitting in the lotus position not meditating. Meditating, it seems, is very relaxing.

Follow-up tests of meditating yogis conducted at the All-

India Institute of Medical Science revealed some other interesting aspects of meditation. The yogis, though wide awake, were able to shut out the external world during periods of meditation. Normally, when someone is sitting quietly with closed eyes and registering a regular alpha rhythm on the EEG, a soft noise nearby will break the alpha rhythm—it is what scientists call the "startle reaction." Yet a number of soft, but clearly audible sounds did not break the alpha pattern of the meditating yogis. The same yogis sitting quietly but not meditating showed the standard startle reaction to noise.

The yogis had always said that they could block external stimuli while still conscious, but Westerners had been disinclined to believe them. The startle reaction seemed to be a totally involuntary act. While one could be trained to show no outward sign of being disturbed, it had been assumed that you couldn't fool the brain. As it turned out, the yogis could fool the brain.

In 1970, Elmer and Alyce Green worked with Swami Rama, a highly trained and exceptionally cooperative yogi who was able to virtually turn on any brain wave pattern at will. Perhaps his most impressive feat was going into a state that he called "yogi sleep." This was characterized by very slow, high amplitude delta waves. The same sort of waves are seen in the EEG of a deeply sleeping person. Yet Swami Rama was able to hear and remember most of the things that were said to him while he was in this state. For the majority of us things that happen around us while we are deeply asleep or unconscious are lost. But is that because they did not register on our minds, or because we are unable to recall them? Might these hidden memories have some effect upon our waking hours? At present we do not know.

At about the same time the yogis were being tested in

India, Japanese researchers were conducting similar studies on their own native practitioners of meditation. Scientists Akira Kasamatsu and Tomio Hirai used the EEG on forty-eight masters and disciples of Zen meditation. Zen meditation is somewhat different than the meditation practiced by the Indian yogis. The most obvious difference is that the Zen meditator sits with his eyes open. Normally the alpha pattern cannot be produced by a subject with his eyes open. Control subjects who sat quietly in the same position as the Zen meditators showed the normal EEG patterns of a fully awake individual. But after a minute or two of meditating, a regular alpha pattern appeared in the EEGs of the Zen meditators. This pattern grew stronger and slower as the meditation continued, and in the more experienced of the meditators, the even slower theta waves began to show up after about half an hour. Usually theta waves are signs of sleep, or at least drowsiness, yet other measurements showed that the Zen meditators were fully awake.

Another intriguing difference between Zen meditation and the meditation of the yogis was in the response to outside stimuli. The yogis had shown no response whatsoever to mild stimuli—they had blocked them out entirely. The Japanese investigators tested their meditators with a series of twenty soft clicks repeated at regular fifteen-second intervals. The meditators reacted, not outwardly, but the clicks produced a momentary disruption in their alpha rhythm. After a few seconds regular alpha was reestablished just as if nothing had happened. This same reaction was produced to all the clicks in the series.

Not only was this type of reaction in marked contrast to the reactions seen in the yogi meditators, but it was also quite different from the reactions of a series of control subjects. The controls sat with their eyes closed in order to develop well-defined alpha rhythms. The first click completely blocked the alpha waves as the controls exhibited a strong startle reaction. But the control subjects quickly became habituated to the noise, and by the fourth click the startle reaction had disappeared entirely. The Zen meditators did not block the stimulus, but they did not show a strong startle reaction, and they did not ever become habituated to it.

The meditators themselves were entirely conscious of what was happening. In their report Kasamatsu and Hirai stated:

"The Zen masters reported to us that they had more clearly perceived each stimulus than in their ordinary waking state. In [the meditative] state of mind, one cannot be affected by either external or internal stimulus, nevertheless he is able to respond to it. He perceives the object, responds to it, and yet is never disturbed by it. Each stimulus is accepted as stimulus itself and treated as such. One Zen master described such a state of mind as that of noticing every person one sees on the street but of not looking with emotional curiosity."

Zen meditation was quite different from yoga meditation, and both were quite different from the states of consciousness which untrained people can attain. It is clear that our previous ideas about what is "normal" human consciousness have been severely limited by our own cultural bias.

But all of this still seems rather far away from the life of the average person in the West. The next series of experiments, though, really brought meditation home. The subjects being tested were not Indian yogis or Zen monks. They were ordinary Americans who had learned the technique of transcendental meditation, or TM, that was developed by the Maharishi Mahesh Yogi.

The Maharishi's reputation in the West had gone into decline since he had first come into prominence as guru for such luminaries as the Beatles and Mia Farrow. The Beatles abandoned him, and even said a few unkind things about his philosophy. There had been some bad publicity surrounding the Maharishi's apparent wealth. People thought it was both odd and incongruous that a supposedly ascetic holy man was flown around in his own private plane. In a tour of America the Maharishi's squeaky voice and rather querulous manner made him look almost foolish during television interviews.

Most suspect of all, however, was the technique of transcendental meditation itself. It seemed just too easy. Perhaps it offended some deeply held part of the Protestant ethic which taught that if one is to derive great spiritual benefit one must do a great deal of spiritual hard work. Transcendental meditation could be learned in just a few hours, and practiced for a mere half hour to forty minutes a day. Yogis and Zen masters spent years in cold and uncomfortable places learning to meditate. Yet here was a technique that promised essentially the same results almost instantly, and without having to give up any of the accustomed comforts of Western life. It sounded just like one of those weight loss systems that is supposed to have pounds "melt away" without resort to the discomforts of dieting or exercise. In short, it sounded phony.

The Maharishi himself is hardly a simple holy man. Aside from having extensive training as a yogi and living in a Himalayan cave for two years, he also holds a degree in physics, and is thoroughly familiar with Western society and Western business techniques. His goals, outlined in several long and rather obscure books, appear cosmic—no less than the spiritual transformation of humanity. But he is also an immensely practical man, and if this transformation is to occur in the West as well as the East, Western methods must be adopted. Important to any spiritual discipline of this type is the role of the guru or teacher. But since most of the teachers will not have spent years meditating in a cave, what they teach must be simple, direct and easily understood. The instructions given to those who wish to teach the Maharishi's techniques sound very much like the instructions given to apprentice Fuller Brush men: "It is better to refrain from using 'you,' 'your' or 'I.' Whenever possible, use 'we' or 'our.' " There is an impressive, efficient and tightly controlled bureaucracy for the spread of the Maharishi's teachings. *Psychology Today* editor Colin Campbell complained, "If the light of the Being glorifies the field of everyday human actions, as the Maharishi has written, then how come these dedicated meditators sound like the phone company?"

All in all the Maharishi's popularity among those normally interested in Oriental religions is not high. He is considered shallow and commercial. But his success among the general population is impressive and growing. According to the Maharishi's organization in Los Angeles, 300,000 Americans have learned his technique of transcendental meditation, and 15,000 more start TM every month. The course is short, simple and costs only $75. It consists of a few lectures and some individual instruction. During the course the meditator is given a secret Sanskrit *mantra* to think about while meditating. The *mantra* is his and his alone and is supposed to be revealed to no one. According to the Maharishi this simple technique should lead to "absolute bliss consciousness," and while many dedicated meditators would deny that they had achieved such a state, most appear to feel that they at least got their $75 worth.

The technique of TM consists basically of having the meditator sit comfortably with eyes closed and bringing to mind the *mantra*. He does not concentrate on the *mantra* or any other thought, and does not try to exclude any either.

But he does avoid following a particular "train of thought" or trying to arrive at any conclusions. Rather the mind is allowed to wander freely. This is not nearly as easy as it sounds and some people find it quite impossible. But most of those who take up the training seem able to master TM rather quickly.

Because TM was so simple and easy to learn, scientists believed investigation of meditators trained in it would be most fruitful. Robert K. Wallace and Herbert Benson of the Harvard Medical School chose thirty-six American volunteers who had been trained in TM by the International Meditation Society based in Los Angeles.

The meditators themselves reported that while meditating they felt in a "profound state of rest." They said that they felt deeply relaxed and free from anxiety. These were subjective judgments, but surprisingly enough the researchers' instruments appeared to back them up. Alpha activity began to show up on the EEG almost as soon as meditation began. The heartbeat slowed down, oxygen consumption decreased by about 17 percent and the electrical resistance of the skin rose sharply. There was also a sharp decline in the amount of a substance called lactate in the blood. A high concentration of lactate in the blood appears to be correlated with a high level of anxiety. Wallace and Benson concluded that all of these readings indicated a general "quiescence of the sympathetic nervous system."

It must be pointed out that not all of these findings have been confirmed by other studies. It must also be noted that researchers who are enthusiastic about TM tend to get more spectacular results than those less involved in the subject. Wallace, who first brought TM to the attention of the scientific community with his doctoral thesis on the physiology of meditation published in the journal *Science* in 1970, was himself a dedicated meditator, and is now president of the

Maharishi International University. There is no implication that the Wallace and Benson results were necessarily wrong or misinterpreted, merely that the issue is not as clear-cut as meditation enthusiasts would have one believe. This sort of ambiguity is common, almost inevitable in studies that involve human behavior. Still there is general agreement that the nervous system of the meditator is somewhat quieter than that of the nonmeditator.

Okay, so what? When we feel threatened, our whole body mobilizes to meet that threat. Our heart rate increases, oxygen consumption goes up, adrenalin pours into the bloodstream, and so forth. We are all ready to either fight or run —this is the so-called "fight flight syndrome." It was a reaction that was quite appropriate for our distant ancestors, who really did have to either fight or run when faced with a critical physical threat. But it is often inappropriate today.

When the boss yells at us, we feel threatened, and the involuntary fight flight reaction takes hold. Yet we are not (usually) going to punch the boss in the nose, nor are we going to run screaming out of the office. Mostly we stand there and take it, and all of the fight flight mobilization is useless and worse, because it puts the body under considerable stress. Moreover, in modern society many face this kind of stress frequently, and it has been implicated in a large number of diseases, everything from asthma to ulcers.

Benson and Wallace noted that the state of the meditator appeared to be the exact opposite of the state of an individual in the grip of the fight flight syndrome. If the fight flight reactions result in harmful stress, then its opposite should result in helpful rest. Wallace and Benson concluded, "It should be well worthwhile to investigate the possibilities for clinical application of this state of wakeful rest and relaxation."

Since their initial report Wallace and Benson and others

have investigated such possibilities, and the results have been encouraging. Wallace and Benson found that regular use of TM appeared to decrease the blood pressure of hypertensive subjects. Other researchers found TM helpful in the treatment of asthma, and that it even helped reduce inflammation in swollen gums.

One psychiatrist reported that patients who took up meditation appeared to improve more rapidly than nonmeditating patients. Meditators showed significantly less hostility than nonmeditators on standard psychological tests.

Both the subjective reports of the meditators and the objective measurements of the scientists indicate that the primary benefit of transcendental meditation is a lessening of anxiety. The usual method of reducing anxiety in our society is through the use of drugs, alcohol and tobacco. A natural line of research would be to discover what effect the regular use of meditation would have on users of these substances. Several studies turned up really spectacular results. Wallace and Benson followed 1,862 subjects who had in one way or another been involved with drugs. They found that those who took up and stuck with the practice of TM dramatically reduced their own use of drugs, alcohol and tobacco, and most actively tried to discourage others from taking up drugs.

These results have substantially been supported by other studies. W. T. Winquist of the University of California at Los Angeles examined the relationship between TM and drug use. He found that after at least three months of TM, 84 percent had considerably reduced their use of marijuana and only about 1.5 percent had increased the use of the drug while on TM.

Winquist found that about half of those in his study said that they had quit or cut down using marijuana because meditation had made their life more serene and fulfilling. In a number of other studies subjects reported themselves to be more relaxed, organized and mature after taking up meditation. Of course, simply sitting down quietly twice a day may reduce stress and the desire for drugs. Even this mild discipline would provide an anchor for an unstable life.

Still it appears that meditation, once thought to be the sole province of mystics and quacks, has attracted increasing scientific interest and respectability. There was a special symposium on the psychology of meditation at the 1973 meeting of the American Psychological Association. Edward Taub, chairman of the symposium, observed that while subjective reports on the value of meditation had been around for a long time, "Our traditions of thought . . . compel us to seek verification of the self-reports through more objective measures." To a great extent it appears that physiological testing has been able to confirm many of these reports.

The potential use of a technique like transcendental meditation is enormous. It holds out the possibility of being able to reduce stress and anxiety without resort to drugs of any kind. Instead of taking a pill or drink in order to wind down, a person might need only to sit quietly and meditate for twenty minutes. With biofeedback training an individual might reach the meditative state more quickly and hold it more easily and surely than is now possible even with TM training. In addition to being a tension-reducing technique, meditation may also result in profound enough changes in an individual's basic reactions that the tension levels no longer build up as they once did—it can prevent stress as well as alleviating it.

But it would be premature, indeed dishonest, to promise that meditation in any of its forms is about to bring to pass a drugless, drinkless, stress-free millennium filled with self-confident, self-fulfilled individuals. The scientific evidence regarding the benefits of meditation is not altogether clear. And one need only look at nations like India in which meditation is widely practiced to see that the millennium is not necessarily the result.

The most obvious problem is that those who take up meditation in the first place may not be a representative cross section of drug users, hypertensives, asthmatics, anxiety-prone individuals or of any of the other groups that have apparently been helped by the practice. The mere fact that they chose meditation and stuck to it may indicate a particular type of physical makeup or personality that allows meditation to work in the first place. There is some evidence that any other relaxing technique would work equally well with such individuals. Those who drop out of the meditation program receive no residual benefits from the training. There is no reliable information on what percentage of the general population can stick with meditation in the first place.

Leon S. Otis and his associates from the Stanford Research Institute divided volunteers into three groups. One group learned TM, another sat quietly each day and repeated a "mock mantra" while a third did not change the pattern of their daily lives at all. Other data was collected from meditators and from individuals who had dropped out of the program. The conclusion of these studies was that people who took up meditation and stuck to it were markedly different in personality from those who cared little for it, or could not stay with the program.

Wrote Otis, "Those who quit meditating, for example, seem to fall into two categories: people with problems too serious to respond to a technique as mild as TM, and people whose personalities are already too well-integrated . . . An extremely anxious person who has managed to restrain his anxiety may find that the deep calm of mantra meditation 'liberates' nothing but problems." He noted that some of the subjects in the test had to drop out when stricken with depression, ulcers or other classical psychosomatic symptoms. But Otis's conclusion was that TM helps more people than it hurts. "The only difference is that when TM works well, it's working on *another type of person* than the one who finds it useless or detrimental. This type of person is probably common in our society—someone reasonably well-integrated, and yet bothered by neurotic anxieties, guilts, and phobias." Otis also found that control subjects who simply sat quietly for fifteen or twenty minutes reported many of the same benefits as did the meditators.

Harvard psychologist Gary Schwartz suggests that there might be some sort of evolutionary precedent for TM. "Meditative practices have existed for thousands of years. Very broadly, we may think of meditation as an act of sustained self-reflection; in this sense it is a natural act. I suspect that there is an evolutionary precedent for meditation. Primitive human societies and even certain apes typically spend part of each day sitting quietly, in what appears to be self-reflection. Who is to say they're not meditating? There may be a basic human need for something like TM."

Yet TM, like a lot of good and needed ideas, may face serious problems when applied on a mass scale. Take, for example, weight reduction programs, surely something needed in American society.

There are many excellent and not terribly difficult diets that will allow fat people to lose weight, if the people could stick to them. But most fat people can't stick to the diets and so remain fat. Smokers face an identical problem. They know they should stop, and there are dozens of systems for doing so. These systems do work for some people, but most smokers can't stop, no matter what technique they try. It has been estimated that about 20 percent of those who enroll in anti-smoking programs stop smoking. All programs have about the same rate of success.

Persistent results of this type have led researchers to try to probe more deeply into the physiology and psychology of obesity and smoking, to try to find out why so many people can't stick to programs, and to devise programs they can stick to.

Another problem is that while meditation itself has been around for centuries, study of it has not. Even in those cases where meditation has been successful, we cannot be sure that the desirable effects will be long-range. Many other self-improvement programs appear to succeed wonderfully for the first year or two, and then begin to break down for the majority of those enrolled. In the first flush of enthusiasm the programs of Alcoholics Anonymous or the drug treatment approach of SYNANON appeared to have been cure-alls. They proved to be useful in some cases, but failed to live up to advance billing. Many alcoholics and drug users try such programs but get no benefit from them, or only temporary benefit. Only time and thorough follow-up studies will provide an adequate picture of the long-range benefits of meditation.

And there is an even trickier problem. Is it the technique of meditation itself or something else which produces these beneficial effects? Medical research has to contend with the placebo effect. We will discuss this in greater detail later, but briefly the placebo effect is what happens when a particular drug or treatment works because the patient thinks it will work, rather than because of any inherent quality of the treatment or drug itself.

Physicians often give patients impressively colored but

useless pills, because the patient wants a pill and believes in the effectiveness of pills. Nevertheless, such dummy pills very often are as good or better at reducing symptoms than a drug. Thus it is possible that a simple belief in meditation, particularly at this moment when there is a great deal of publicity and enthusiasm surrounding the technique, may be the real basis for the beneficial results. When the publicity wears off, the beneficial results of meditation may also melt away.

The researcher himself may be the focus of the placebo effect. It has long been known that doctors who are enthusiastic about a particular treatment are likely to get better results with it than doctors who are skeptical. The patient feels better simply because the doctor is paying sympathetic attention to him and providing him with the hope that he is going to get better. Thus Wallace, who is quite interested in the subject, tends to get better results than less sympathetic experimenters.

All of this seems to indicate that what might be called the "meditation effect" is a good deal more complex than the early experimental results would lead one to believe.

I am in no sense trying to deny the possible importance of the findings about meditation. They are, as Taub says, "suggestive and exciting." But I am attempting to warn against overenthusiasm. Overenthusiasm can lead to disappointment, and quite possibly to a situation where ultimately one throws the baby out with the bathwater. One needs only to recall the melancholy history of hypnotism to see what can happen. At first hypnotism was greeted with enormous enthusiasm as a possible cure for all the world's ills. But it couldn't deliver on such a promise and the practice soon fell into the hands of fools or, worse, outright charlatans. Physicians and scientists, who tend to be conservative in such matters, fled the scene in horror. Even today the practice has not quite been able to shed its aura of being just a bit shady.

While practitioners of TM have made little of alpha waves, and positively scorn the idea of biofeedback (who needs a machine when you can learn to meditate in a few hours anyway?), the fact that high alpha production is a characteristic of meditation, and that alpha production has been learned through biofeedback inevitably links the three in the public mind. It has been suggested that an easier and deeper form of meditation can be learned through the use of biofeedback equipment.

Naturally the hucksters have already begun to move in. The most obvious exploitation is in the sale of a variety of feedback devices that can run anywhere from $100 to over $1000. The major problem is that even if the machine works as it is supposed to, and there is absolutely no guarantee that it will work at all, the average person will not know how to operate it properly without a good deal of instruction. This sort of instruction is not readily available.

The EEG is a sensitive and complicated instrument, and there are many ways in which it can give an incorrect reading. Blinking, forehead twitching, eyeball rolling and even teeth gritting can produce an alpha-like reading for the unwary user. An unfortunate subject who thinks that he is reinforcing his alpha state may in reality be simply reinforcing a facial tic—hardly the desired result.

Besides the EEG machine are a variety of other devices that may measure anything from muscle tension to Lord knows what. For example, a large circulation occult magazine advertises a "Cybertronic Detector" with "Resistive Feedback," but just what it is supposed to detect, the ad does not say. There are even machines which are supposed to deliver a small electrical current to the head, exactly the opposite of what biofeedback is all about, yet they attempt to cash in on the popularity of the biofeedback idea. Government agencies have made little attempt to regulate such devices, probably because the laws are rather vague.

In most cases, aside from being a waste of money, such machines probably do no great harm. They are almost all battery-powered, so the user can't electrocute himself even if he tries. Simply getting hooked up to the machine, whether it is working properly or not, may help to propel a trusting soul into a restful and relaxed state—the placebo effect again. But not everyone finds alpha pleasurable. In a minority of subjects the alpha state is experienced as one of frustration such an individual might experience increased anxiety and psychosomatic symptoms after fooling around with alpha feedback. Still, since most of the home machines work so poorly, there is little danger even for such individuals.

There is another aspect of alpha which may have more long-range consequences. There is at least some indication that alpha is associated with low achievement. One study has shown that poor students can attain the alpha state more easily than good students. Is it possible that the relaxed detachment so often associated with alpha might indicate or lead to passive acceptance of one's state, to what theologian Reinhold Niebuhr once called the "tendency to flee the responsibilities of history and engage in premature adventures into eternity"?

A similar problem has arisen in relation to TM. According to the Maharishi, meditation increases "creative intelligence." That is quite a broad term, and both intelligence and creativity are extremely hard to measure, still some attempts have been made. Harvard's Schwartz gave a battery of standard creativity tests to sixteen meditators and sixteen nonmeditators. The meditators got consistently lower scores, though they appeared to be trying harder. Yet on other kinds of creativity tests, particularly those involving free association, meditators got higher scores.

Schwartz concluded that "TM may enhance the germinal stages of creativity, but if practiced to excess, it may reduce the chance of the meditator's producing a recognizably creative product."

No one has any idea whether meditation can increase intelligence, but psychologist William Linden found that third-graders trained in meditation were less anxious when taking tests. There is a good deal of evidence to indicate that the less anxious person will think and act more effectively.

This entire issue is potentially an explosive one, for it calls forth all the old stereotypes of the "passive" Oriental and the "active" Westerner. Even technicians like Kamiya tend to view their findings in terms of some sort of East-West conflict. Kamiya has written:

"Western man has tended to focus on the external world, assuming the internal world to be beyond control, except for what happens to it as a result of efforts toward goal achievement in the external world. Eastern man, on the other hand, appears to have focused more attention on achievements (knowledge and control) in his internal world, assuming the external world to be largely beyond control."

Will society or the individual benefit from turning technology inward? Some studies indicate that artists and musicians are exceptionally good at producing alpha. Kamiya noted that he finds high alpha producers more likable than those who find alpha difficult. Are alpha-prone people more "sensitive," "creative," and "freer," but less likely to succeed in the drudgery of schoolwork? It is really pointless to speculate yet, for we know so little.

In any case the individual contemplating the purchase of

an alpha feedback device need not worry that his alpha training will make him passive, nor should he believe that it will make him creative. Despite the promises, overt and implied, most of these machines don't do much of anything.

Another offshoot of the current interest in biofeedback, alpha, meditation, et cetera, is the proliferation of "mind control" courses. These courses are offered under a variety of names, but the pattern is fairly standard. The mind control instructor sets up temporary shop in a particular area, rents a meeting room in a local motel and saturates the area with newspaper advertisements extolling the wonders of the system that he teaches.

The ads, as well as the introductory lecture and other promotional material, hint that not only tranquility, but fantastic psychic powers lie within the grasp of anyone who completes the course.

The courses themselves are a good deal older in content than all of the up-to-date jargon of the come-on pitch would lead one to suspect. In the first place, few if any of the major courses employ any type of feedback equipment. They are primarily mixtures of positive thinking, "new age" occultism, hypnotism and a good bit of yoga and Oriental philosophy. Some mind control sellers have been accused of making vague promises about curing cancer and other diseases, which is a dangerous and thoroughly disreputable practice. Most courses, however, steer clear of such promises, and do no particular harm. They may even do a bit of good. At least they give people who are bored, lonely, and unhappy something to occupy their time for a little while, and some hope that they can do something about their troubles.

The primary objection one can raise to the courses, aside from the fact that they really have little to do with the newer findings about meditation or biofeedback, which probably attracted an individual to the course in the first place, is that they are expensive. Courses can run from one hundred to several hundred dollars. This is often more than the "student" can really afford, and mind control instructors are not shy about dunning slow-paying students. Many of the instructors of these courses are basically salesmen and in the past have been involved in selling such things as encyclopedias and health spa memberships. Typically the instructor operates on a franchise from one of the major "mind control" organizations. He turns back in the neighborhood of 30 percent of his receipts to the national organization, but the remaining profit must be substantial, judging from the way in which this particular activity has proliferated in the past few years.

Perhaps the best analogy to these mind control courses are the various dance courses—they are high pressure and just a wee bit shady. Although one may learn to dance from them, the cost seems too high for the value received.

But whether the people who run these various courses are sincere or not, most of the "graduates" appear to believe that they have benefited greatly from the course. Those who drop out are naturally less enthusiastic, and some rather bitter. Graduates, however, are the best salesmen for the courses. Those I have talked to have the zeal of new converts, and claim, apparently with great feeling, that they now possess a whole range of psychic powers, though they are often a bit unclear as to what the powers are supposed to be. My experience has been that those who go the whole route with mind control training are generally persons who have had a previous interest in, and contact with, psychic and occult subjects. Although I cannot claim to have met a representative sample of mind control course graduates, I would think it very likely that this kind of background was common.

MIND MEDITATION AND MACHINE

Some mind control graduates are so convinced of their powers that they practically beg to be tested, something that no conscious fraud is likely to do unless he is confident that he can control the conditions of the test.

Graduates of the course called Silva Mind Control are supposed to be able to make a distant clairvoyant diagnosis of a physically ill person. The graduates claim that they know what disease a person has after receiving only the first name, last initial, sex, age and city of residence of the person. (Medical clairvoyance is an old practice, and one that from time to time has enjoyed great popularity in the United States. What this has to do with biofeedback or alpha is unclear. A variety of dissimilar but vaguely occult practices are all mixed together in such courses.) Making a successful distant clairvoyant diagnosis is one of the tests in the Silva Mind Control course final exam.

Several studies have been conducted by parapsychologists to test the powers of clairvoyant diagnosis claimed by Silva graduates. What is most significant is that the Silva graduates not only willingly participated in the tests, but in one case practically forced the test to be held. The graduates were given the required information about various ill persons, and their diagnoses were submitted to the doctors who had supplied the patients' names. In one study the diagnoses of the Silva graduate showed virtually no correspondence with the true condition of the patients. In another study one graduate out of the ten tested appeared to do slightly better than chance on his diagnosis. Since these tests were also carried out by people who would tend to believe, if not in Silva Mind Control, at least in distant clairvoyant diagnosis, mind control enthusiasts can take little comfort from the results.

More bizarre yet are the various alpha and feedback "churches" mentioned at the beginning of this chapter. Actually it is difficult to know whether such developments are serious or not. Underground newspapers occasionally carry ads that offer mail-order certificates of ordination as a priest of such institutions as "The Feedback Church of America."

It would seem that tuning in on one's own brain waves should be the most solitary of human activities. Yet British psychologist Christopher Jones reports, "Stories even circulate of feedback orgies, with whole groups of individuals of *both sexes* linked to each other's alpha machines, enjoying the thrill and challenge of manipulating each other's brain waves. In fact the latest trend is very definitely away from solitary exploration of the phenomena into real group activities . . ."

The easy passage from alpha feedback and TM to religion should surprise no one. Only in our hurried modern society has meditation been regarded as a possible temporary relaxer. Traditionally meditation has been a part of religion in both East and West.

The goal of Zen meditation is the state called *satori,* and it is the word most commonly used by modern Western meditators. But there are other states of higher inner awareness that are reached through other forms of meditation. Will biofeedback provide a quick entry through these fabled doors as well?

In an essay on meditation and feedback Durand Kiefer suggests, "Perhaps within another decade the number of alpha-masters, theta-masters and delta-masters living among us may exceed the number of Zen-masters, Yoga-masters, and sufi-masters who have lived since time began."

Says Kamiya, "I do think . . . it will be possible to find the unique neurophysiological signature of meditation by checking out other channels—besides alpha. Once we have the complete physiological pattern that characterizes meditation, there's no reason why we can't train people, with feedback, to mimic it in a relatively short space of time."

Purists, on the other hand, argue that while feedback training may allow a subject to mimic some of the meditative states, there is no shortcut to the higher states of awareness, and to think that there is merely displays our Western prejudices and ignorance.

Another pertinent question is, Do we really want to attain these higher states of meditation at all? Though, like all spiritual or mystic experiences, the highest states of meditation defy description, they appear to involve a total loss of self, and a sort of "blank mind" state. Medieval Christian mystics have tried to describe "the Cloud of Unknowing" which was then the goal of meditation. One experimenter with alpha feedback thought he had come close to the higher states of consciousness when he achieved a state of mind "like a flowing grey-black film with a luminous quality." Perhaps the state achieved with feedback is lacking something essential, and perhaps this final goal of meditation is not a worthwhile one in the first place.

Perhaps *satori* or the Maharishi's state of "pure consciousness" is not as unique and mysterious as the cosmic rhetoric makes them sound. Psychologist Robert Ornstein has suggested that when a person concentrates on a single stimulus, like the *mantra,* it seems eventually to disappear, leaving pure attention but without content. Ornstein believes that studies indicate this is a basic physiological reaction of the brain. People will react the same way to any unobjectionable but repetitive stimulus. Concentrating on the single object first reduces a person's attention to other stimuli, and then, with repetition, vanishes itself, leaving awareness of nothing in particular. Put that way, this "higher state of consciousness," sounds a good deal less attractive than when described by meditation enthusiasts.

3
DOING THE IMPOSSIBLE

For well over a century now, Westerners have been alternately intrigued and skeptical of reports coming out of the East, particularly India, of holy men who could do all sorts of "impossible" things. Many of the more spectacular feats, like walking across beds of hot coals, presented Western science with no basic problems. For example, psychologist Theodore X. Barber proposed that certain yogis can walk across hot coals because they have developed hard calluses on their feet, take powerful pain-killing drugs such as heroin, and walk very fast. Others have suggested that the coals are not nearly as hot as they look and experienced and confident fire walkers are nothing more than well-trained performers.

The yogis who reclined on beds of nails or stuck themselves full of pins, or stood on one foot for months or years on end, were displaying remarkable physical control, but there was nothing in Western physiological theory that held such feats were impossible. Indeed, the West has had its own ascetic saints who rivaled the most ingenious yogis in mortification of the flesh. Training or physiological type allows certain individuals to endure or block levels of pain most of

DOING THE IMPOSSIBLE

us would find utterly unbearable.

The "impossible" yoga feats, as far as Western science was concerned, were not necessarily the showy ones, they were the feats that involved control over the involuntary bodily functions—heartbeat, blood pressure, digestion, and the like.

Until recently most scientists believed that the human body contained two distinct nervous systems. One was controlled by the outer brain through a system of nerves that ran down the center of the spinal column. This nervous system gives us voluntary control of the muscles which move our arms, legs, eyeballs, et cetera.

The second system, centered in the lower brain, is called the autonomic nervous system. The nerves of this system travel down the sides of the spinal cord and regulate basic bodily functions—like the beating of the heart and functioning of other internal organs. Even the muscles controlled by the two systems look different. The involuntary muscles are called smooth, while the voluntary muscles are called striated, for they show regular stripe-like markings under the microscope. It was assumed that the voluntary nervous system was under the control of the conscious mind, and the autonomic nervous system was not. The autonomic nervous system could be profoundly affected by our emotions, which were also beyond our direct conscious control.

For a long time doctors have been able to monitor the heart rate, blood pressure and other internal functions. If something went wrong, the doctors tried to correct it with drugs or surgery. There was no belief that the patient himself could, by his own volition, correct any malfunctions. But if yogis and others could indeed control the involuntary functions, this might have profound implications for medical science.

Moreover, the implications went beyond the medical—

they hinted that human consciousness was a good deal more important than most Western thinking had hitherto allowed. If man could consciously do "impossible" things with his body, perhaps consciousness could achieve other equally impossible feats.

For a long time there had been intriguing hints even in the West that the distinction between the two nervous systems might not be as sharp as commonly believed. A magician like Harry Houdini was able to swallow a key, and then bring it up at will, thus reversing the normally "involuntary" process of swallowing. The actress Sarah Bernhardt was supposed to be able to produce tears at will, thus exercising voluntary control over another supposedly involuntary activity—crying. But such apparent control was generally viewed as part of a performance, a trick, and thus not to be taken very seriously.

As early as 1935, Therese Brosse went to India with a portable electrocardiograph and claimed that she found a yogi who could stop his heart. It was widely assumed that her equipment was not working properly.

By the late 1950s, though, both Western and Indian investigators began more extensive and careful investigations of the yogis' claims. It wasn't an easy task, for many of the yogis were deeply religious men who were not interested in proving anything, particularly if it meant being hooked up to a variety of measuring gadgets bristling with wires and dials. Physical yoga, or Hatha yoga, is not merely a series of exotic exercises aimed at bodily control. It is one path by which the yogi attempts to liberate his spirit from the material world. Such men are not interested in making the *Guiness Book of World Records* or being listed in medical texts.

However, among the yogis are some who are essentially performers who make their living by displaying their physical prowess. Some may have feared that their claims of exceptional powers might somehow be exposed. But eventually a sufficient number of cooperative subjects were found. The results of a long series of tests conducted by Marion A. Wenger of UCLA and Basu K. Bagchi of the University of Michigan Medical School were both fascinating and ambiguous.

Several of the yogis they tested with sophisticated monitoring equipment had claimed that they were able to stop their hearts from beating. During such periods there was no detectable pulse at the wrist or anywhere else, nor could a heartbeat be heard with a stethoscope. But Wenger and Bagachi had an electrocardiogram, or EKG, which measures the electrical activity of the heart. According to the EKG, the yogis' hearts went right on pumping during the periods in which they were supposed to have stopped.

What the yogis had accomplished, through a combination of controlled breathing and muscular contractions, was to squeeze their veins practically shut. Thus the heart had little or no blood to pump, and its actions were undetectable by ordinary means. This was an impressive feat of control of the voluntary muscles, but it did not represent control of the involuntary heart muscle.

However, one of the subjects was a yogi who said that while he could not stop his heart altogether, he could slow it down, and that is exactly what he did. He slowed his heartbeat from 73 to 24 beats a minute. If the "involuntary" bodily functions like the heartbeat were not subject to conscious control this should have been impossible, yet there it was.

In follow-up experiments Wenger and Bagchi found several other yogis who could slow their heartbeats for a few seconds. This brought up the interesting possibility that a yogi with sufficient training and talent could simply will himself to die. There had been numerous tales of yogis who had expressed a desire to "leave the body" and then simply did so while meditating amid a group of disciples. This was not a case in which a sick person had lost the "will to live" but rather a case in which a healthy person had acquired a "will to die."

One yogi showed the experimenters that he was able to sweat on command. He said that he had learned this while practicing in a Himalayan cave. The extreme cold bothered him, so his teacher told him to concentrate on hot weather scenes. After some months of practice he was able to feel more comfortable. But when he used the same technique in warmer climates, he not only felt hot, he began to sweat.

Among the more lurid tales to emerge from India were those of yogis who were buried alive for days or even weeks, but emerged from their graves perfectly healthy. Westerners greeted such tales with considerable skepticism. The assumption was that some sort of trick was involved. The graves in which the yogis were buried were not airtight. There would have been some seepage of air from the surface, so that the buried yogis would not have to accomplish the absolutely supernatural feat of existing for weeks without any oxygen at all. Still, unless there was some form of deliberate fakery involved (a hidden air hose from the surface, for example), the amount of air reaching the buried yogi would have been well below the minimum amount required by a normal waking or sleeping person.

Dr. Bal K. Anad, chairman of the Physiology Department of the All-India Institute of Medical Science in New Delhi, conducted an experiment with one yogi who claimed he could be buried alive. The yogi was sealed inside an airtight glass box while a host of his physiological functions were

DOING THE IMPOSSIBLE

monitored through electrical leads. The yogi was able to slow down his basal metabolic rate, a measure which determines the amount of oxygen the body needs, by one half. The drop was considered utterly astonishing considering that in a normal person the basal metabolism rate rarely drops more than 10 percent even in deepest sleep. Since the box was airtight, the yogi was released before the oxygen fell to a dangerously low level, but the clear message of the experiment was that the stories about yogis being buried and emerging unharmed were to some extent true. They could not live without oxygen entirely, but they could survive with far less than once believed possible.

All of this was quite fascinating. It proved that despite all the Western sneers at Indian "fake fakirs," these men really had achieved remarkable control of their bodies, and could do a lot of things once believed impossible. Most significantly the experiments indicated that the dividing line between the voluntary and autonomic nervous system was not nearly as sharp as it had seemed. More conventional laboratory studies with animals tended to support the same conclusion.

The potential of such findings was enormous. Irregular heartbeats could be corrected by a sheer act of will. Blood pressure could be lowered without drugs. Even the production of errant glands might someday be brought under conscious control. That was the promise anyway.

The problem was finding a way to apply these findings about yogis to Western society. The yogis undergo years of rigorous training and discipline. A once-a-week yoga class at the local "Y" may make one feel good for a while, but it is not the same thing at all.

Yoga, as we noted, is not merely a program of exotic physical exercises. It is a religious discipline that grew from an ancient and extremely complex set of beliefs that are utterly alien to Western thought. While all Indians are by no means yogis, Indian society at large shares the beliefs on which yoga is based. A man who spends years meditating in a cave in India may be regarded as holy. In the West he would be regarded as a lunatic, or at best someone who was "wasting his time." Most Westerners would undoubtedly count a lifetime of such training as too high a price to pay even for greater control over the autonomic nervous system and the improved health that goes with it.

But is there any way of achieving yogi-like control without having to go through the rigors of yoga discipline? The answer is a qualified yes. It is the technique that we have come to call biofeedback. Yogis spend a great deal of time in quiet solitude simply becoming aware of what is going on inside of them. If we are to control what is happening inside, we must first know that something is actually happening. We in the West are so involved with the outside world, our senses are so assailed by stimuli, that we fail to pick up clues to our internal state that the yogis can recognize. At moments of extreme quiet we may become acutely, even alarmingly, aware of the beating of our own hearts or the sounds of our stomach at work. But such moments are increasingly rare in the harried modern world. Biofeedback may be a way of quickly learning some of these clues, and that is the necessary first step toward control.

Typical of the clinical applications of biofeedback was a program carried out by Drs. Bernard Engel and Theodore Weiss. The doctors concentrated on training patients to voluntarily control the supposedly involuntary beating of the heart.

As subjects the doctors had eight patients who suffered from cardiac arrhythmias—serious irregularities in the normal pumping rhythm of the heart. In a typical training session the patient lay in a hospital bed with EKG electrodes taped to his chest. The signals controlled a light panel that bore a similarity to a traffic signal. When a green light came on, the patient was supposed to make his heart beat faster. When a red light came on, he was supposed to slow down his heart. The yellow light signaled that he was "on the road" and his heart was beating normally. The patient was supposed to keep the yellow light on as long as possible. This light was the "reward" or "reinforcement" for the training. For the seriously ill person any sign that he is better provides a tremendous boost, thus the yellow light not only let the patient know when his heart was beating normally but also gave him an incentive to keep it beating that way.

Engel and Weiss found that five of their eight patients had succeeded in controlling their heartbeats to some extent. The most successful subject was a woman with a long history of heart trouble. She showed such a marked improvement that she was able to stop taking the drugs previously required to control her heart, and remained free of serious symptoms for two years.

What did voluntary control of the heart "feel like" and how did the patients actually exercise this control? Here the patients' descriptions of their own state of mind were inconsistent. One woman, for example, "thought about relaxing" but this speeded up her heart and stabilized it.

The point is that the biofeedback training process appears to work for some people. The problem is that it is no easy cure-all. Each patient in the Engel and Weiss study received at least fifty training sessions, and the sessions averaged around eighty minutes each. A good deal of sophisticated equipment as well as trained workers were needed. Such therapy would be extremely expensive and relatively few hospitals would be equipped to offer it at present. And we still do not know what the long-term effects of such training may be.

While some people with high blood pressure or irregular heart rhythms have been trained to produce more normal readings under controlled conditions, so far doctors have had relatively little success in having the benefits of the training carry beyond the laboratory situation. For most patients this method of control appears to break down when they return to the pressures and distractions of normal day-to-day life.

The apparent success of the biofeedback technique may be due as much to "faith" as to anything else. The yogi is able to accomplish otherwise impossible feats because he is sustained by his beliefs. We Westerners do not share the yogi's beliefs, but we do believe in something—we believe in machines. In addition to informing us as to what is going on inside ourselves, the machine may also serve the same function as the prayer wheel or prayer stick serves in many Eastern religions. It is an object of concentration, a visible symbol of power and a psychological prop for faith. And for many the machines doubtless retain a magical aura, as if somehow the control radiates from the machine rather than from inside the individual.

Control of the internal organs through the use of biofeedback has been called "visceral learning," and support for it has been growing among physicians and research scientists. This represents a tremendous change from a decade ago when the idea of control of the autonomic nervous system seemed impossible. But since the potential of visceral learning is so enormous and so personal, potentially affecting the health of every one of us, responsible scientists are unusually cautious about making startling claims for their success.

And in truth, the caution is well-justified. Still today there exists considerable doubt as to whether such a thing as visceral learning will ever play a major role in the treatment of disease. Experimental results are not entirely unambiguous, and one could even argue that there is no solid proof that visceral learning really takes place to any significant degree. Many scientists still argue that voluntary control of the involuntary nervous system has not been adequately demonstrated. Biofeedback may ultimately produce a revolution in medicine, but the revolution is not here, and it would be both foolish and irresponsible to start proclaiming the dawn of a new era on the basis of what has been accomplished so far.

There is, however, one area in which biofeedback is having an immediate effect: that is in helping us gain better control over the voluntary muscles. If the muscles are voluntary, why do we need biofeedback to gain control over them at all? Because even our voluntary muscles are often out of our control and this loss of control can result in such things as tension headaches, nervous tics, restless nights, and that tight feeling in the back of the neck that one so often gets at the end of a hard day. All of these unpleasant symptoms and many more may appear when the voluntary muscles involuntarily contract in response to stress.

A machine called the electromyograph, or EMG, measures minute changes in muscle tension. As the muscles contract and relax, they produce tiny electrical charges which can be amplified and converted into an audible signal. When muscles begin tensing up, the tone gets louder. And when an individual becomes aware of these contractions, he may be able to learn to control them.

Work with EMG feedback has been going on since the early 1960s, and the results have not only been encouraging, they have been truly dramatic. People who had become virtual invalids because of severe headaches reported themselves to be headache-free for the first time in years after only a dozen or so training sessions. Insomniacs who could not get through a night without sleeping pills were able to throw away their pills and still sleep soundly as a result of EMG training.

Where the limits of this sort of therapy are no one really knows. Dr. George B. Whatmore of Seattle links muscle tension to a huge list of ailments, including such things as depression and circulatory disorders. He believes that most of us have particular muscles which tense up during stress, even when we are not aware that the muscles have contracted. These tensions in turn set off a chain reaction of disturbances throughout our body, Dr. Whatmore contends. The doctor first uses a sensor to try to locate which muscles are tense, and then through feedback training tries to ease the tensions.

While not every researcher would go as far as Dr. Whatmore does in blaming muscular tension for so many human ills, there is general agreement that some of our most common disorders, notably headaches and insomnia, are created by muscle tension and can be aided by training in relaxation through the use of feedback. Says one psychologist who has worked extensively in this area, "I think doctors are going to lend patients an EMG machine instead of handing out sleeping pills in the future."

The history of medical research almost compels caution. There have been numerous apparent "revolutionary breakthroughs" in treatment which somehow or another never panned out. For every penicillin there have been hundreds of dead ends. Yet a few conclusions seem clear: 1. Many of the "involuntary" functions of the body may be under far greater voluntary control than we had suspected. 2. Yogis can do at least some of the things that had been claimed for them. 3. By biofeedback physical control of internal functions may be improved.

But none of the realized or even potential benefits of biofeedback and allied subjects can quite account for the attitude that has developed toward it. These discoveries have philosophical implications that reach to the very core of the question, "What is man?" In the view of materialists, man is the sum total of his heredity and environment. The interaction between these two may be quite complex, but the fact remains that man is a biological machine that can operate only within certain well-defined and quite mechanical limits.

The view was stated most brutally by Harvard psychologist B. F. Skinner in his popular and disturbing book *Beyond Freedom and Dignity*. Skinner says that neither free will nor human dignity are concepts which have any real meaning in the life of the human race. Man can be changed, says Skinner, only by proper conditioning, a kindly sort of conditioning based on rewards rather than punishments, but conditioning nonetheless.

This view that we are in no way the masters of our own fate has been greeted with howls of outrage by those who believe that man is something more than a big-brained, two-legged rat in a psychologist's conditioning box. In the various discoveries that have been lumped together here under the heading biofeedback some believe that they have found an effective argument against this view.

Dr. Elmer Green of the Menninger Foundation, an active researcher into biofeedback, puts the case very strongly. Biofeedback, he says, "implies a revolution in the way we see ourselves and our potentialities, it breaks down the ancient distinctions between 'mind and body.' It implies that we need not be prisoners of our emotions or at the mercy of our physical weakness."

Green has written that if people simply knew that a host

of bodily processes could be influenced by will, many prevailing ideas about physical and mental health would change. "It would then be quite clear and understandable that we are individually responsible to a large extent for our state of health or disease.

"It's hard to describe the impact of people who can do the impossible. Skinner says that if you think you have free will, it is just a perception of the chemicals sloshing around in your head. Then you meet one of those guys who can do impossible things. It makes you think there is something to be learned about a person's ability to be programmed by his genes and his conditioning. You can make a better life for yourself."

And yet, one might argue that biofeedback training itself is merely conditioning at a deeper level and there is nothing in these discoveries that effectively refutes the physiochemical machine model. It is an argument that is likely to be with us for a very long time.

4
FAITH HEALING

IF you have not personally used the services of a faith healer, you probably know of someone who has. The practice of faith healing is extremely ancient, very widespread and astonishingly persistent. Today, with medicine making unprecedented strides, faith healing not only shows no signs of disappearing but it is apparently enjoying a resurgence of popularity and perhaps even gaining new respectability.

Naturally any attempt to evaluate the subject of faith healing presents some extremely difficult problems. First there is the name itself. Many people who are called faith healers actively dislike that description. They say that "faith" has little or nothing to do with the healing process and that healing is a gift from God or the result of the expulsion of demons. Some of the best-known healers of history have been nonbelievers who claimed that they drew their power from the manipulation of some subtle, pervasive, but entirely natural force in the universe. There are even those like the Christian Scientists who object to the whole idea of healing. Illness, they say, is an illusion, therefore one cannot be healed of something that does not exist.

Healers have worked by praying (or occasionally cursing), stroking, laying on of hands (and in one case feet), staring, waving hands or through the agency of an astonishing array of devices, from magnets to boxes that were supposed to capture "healing energies" in the universe. Priests, saints, doctors, beggars, madmen and very often kings have been credited with healing powers. Usually a healer had to touch or at least see the individual he was supposed to be healing, but some of the most successful cures have been credited to absent healing, when patient and healer were separated by hundreds or thousands of miles and often when the patient himself had no idea that he was being healed. While healing is usually associated with individuals, it has also been attributed to places, springs, grottos, trees, churches and tombs and objects like meteorites, precious stones and holy relics.

It is, as you can see, a huge subject, and one not easy to generalize about. Perhaps paranormal healing might be a more accurate description of the phenomena. But even there, objections can be raised. So despite its inadequacy, we will let the term faith healing stand. When the words faith healing are used, most people assume that they apply to the broad range of practices just outlined, and not to any specific school or group which insists that faith on the part of the sufferer or the healer is a necessary prerequisite to cure.

We are not only going to examine the scope of faith healing, but its effectiveness. Does it work? And if it does, how? First, though, a little history of the subject will be useful for us to understand how we came to believe what we do about faith healing.

In ancient times, and among primitive tribes today, there is no real difference between what we might call conventional healing and faith healing.

Scripture credits the Apostles with many "miraculous"

cures, and tradition accords them even more. Apostolic cures were effected by laying on of hands, verbal commands, and it was even said that the shadow of St. Peter could restore health. Healing was done on both an individual and a mass basis. It was considered an integral part of Christianity and there is evidence that in the early Church priests were chosen at least in part for their gifts of healing.

Some historians of religion have speculated that one of the great appeals of early Christianity was its strong healing tradition. Wealthy pagans despised Christians because of their habit of consorting with the sick.

The healing tradition was carried on vigorously throughout the first three centuries of Christianity, but by the fourth century, it began to weaken. Though miracles, healing and otherwise, were supposed to still take place, they were considered less numerous than they once had been. Some theologians began to assert that the time of miracles had passed. Healing was more widely practiced by a variety of sects that orthodox Christians considered heretical.

The conversion of the Roman empire to Christianity resulted in an almost complete decline in the healing tradition. Revelation was complete and disease came to be regarded as a direct expression of God's will. Any attempt to interfere with disease might be deemed ungodly. One might pray for relief of pain, but it was best simply to bear it and concentrate on preparation for the next world. Both paranormal cures and orthodox medicine were discouraged, and occasionally banned entirely. The many hospitals established by the Church were not places where it was expected that the sick would recover. They were places where the sick could prepare for a Christian death.

Healing miracles were still attributed to the relics of saints, and exorcisms, which are the reverse side of the healing coin, were still performed. But in general, whatever healing took place was in the hands of heretical groups, or was carried on in folk tradition by wise men and women, who later came to be regarded as witches.

By the fifteenth century, however, the healing tradition began to revive within the Church. Certain highly regarded holy men, like St. Vincent Ferrer, were reputed to cure many ailments by touch. Relics or shrines of saints gained increasingly great reputations for healing. Indeed it became practically a prerequisite for saintliness that miracle cures should be attributed to relics and shrines associated with an individual. Any person who had a reputation for extreme holiness got the reputation of healer while still alive.

Another tradition that began to revive was the belief that royalty could cure certain ailments. The king was divinely anointed, and it was assumed he possessed special powers. This belief became particularly strong in England, where the king's touch was said to provide a potent cure for scrofula, the "king's evil," a common, ugly and painful skin condition. In the seventeenth century Charles II "touched" an average of five thousand sufferers a year during his reign, and a variety of "touch pieces," rings or coins specially blessed by the king, circulated throughout England and the continent. Sometimes demands for the king's healing services were so great that people were killed in the crush to get near him.

Not all monarchs were impressed by their own reputed healing powers. Queen Elizabeth hated the practice and didn't hold healing services. William III also thought healing foolish, but, when pressed, would perform the ritual gestures, though he is reported to have "blessed" those who came to him with the words "God give you better health and more sense."

From the seventeenth century onwards, however, the most

FAITH HEALING

famous healers were neither saints nor monarchs, but more ordinary folk, who for a variety of reasons came to believe that they had been given the "gift" of healing.

Typical of this type of healer was Valentine Greatrakes, a moderately wealthy Irish magistrate. Around 1663, Greatrakes had "an impulse or strange persuasion" that he possessed healing powers. Over the next few years he treated thousands of individuals for a variety of ailments, and was credited with many remarkable cures, though he admitted that there were also many cases that resisted his ministrations. Greatrakes' technique was to stroke the afflicted part of the sufferer's body and draw out the ailment or its symptoms. For this he was given the title "the Stroker."

Greatrakes rarely took any payment for his services; indeed, his own fortunes suffered as a result of the time he had to spend treating patients. This brings up an interesting point about faith healing. It is a field that would seem almost ready-made for confidence men, yet there appear to have been relatively few, at least among the more famous of healers. Like Greatrakes, most of them took little or nothing for their services, and often exhausted themselves to spread the benefits of the "gift" in which they sincerely believed. Even those who pursued wealth were generally believers in their own powers.

Valentine Greatrakes' powers began to fade after about five years and he gave up healing. He never seemed quite sure just what he had done or why he could no longer do it. He was described as a rather strange man who often talked of demons, and it seems he believed his healing involved some form of exorcism, though in practice it looked more like a traditional laying on of hands.

Prince Alexander von Hohenlohe was a minor German aristocrat who was ordained a priest and discovered his healing gifts quite early in life. The cures attributed to him are typical of many other healers. His method was simply to pray fervently over the sick person, but he did introduce one innovation which was to become highly significant in later years. Von Hohenlohe announced he would pray for the healing of those who wrote to him of their afflictions, no matter where they might be. Requests for prayers flooded in from all over the world.

His most spectacular cure took place in 1826, when the priest prince, without leaving Germany, was supposed to have healed the sister of the mayor of Washington, D.C. She was suffering from almost total paralysis and was at the point of death. The cure was said to have begun at the exact moment when von Hohenlohe was saying a special mass in Germany. Von Hohenlohe was the first to have made extensive use of this method of "absent healing." The priest prince was never able to repeat the spectacular success of his trans-Atlantic cure, and the Church tried to restrict his healing activities somewhat, but twenty years later he was still seeing or praying for thousands of sufferers every year.

Zouave Jacob, who began his career in healing in the mid-1860s, got his nickname because he was a trombonist in the famed military band of the Zouaves. The Zouave became so celebrated that crowds of sick followed him whenever he appeared in public. This created difficulties for the band and he finally had to leave the army.

The Zouave cured patients simply by staring at them. He did not claim 100 percent success, however, and would often dismiss patients by saying, "I can do nothing for your disease." He was generally considered an arrogant and disagreeable fellow, yet he took nothing for his services, and made only a small income from his writings.

The Zouave, at least during his earlier years, was an outspoken agnostic. Later in his healing career, which lasted until his death at the beginning of World War I, he became interested in spiritualism, health foods, and ascribed his powers to "magnetism."

Magnetism takes us back a bit in time to the eighteenth century and to the most famous of all nonreligious healers, Franz Mesmer. His career is far too well known to require any detailed repetition here. It is enough to recall that he flourished first in Austria, and then after a dispute with Austrian physicians, he moved to France, where his cures became all the rage in the years before the French Revolution.

Mesmer did become wealthy from his practice, and he was more than a bit of a showman. He was also egotistical, suspicious, disloyal to friends, a shameless social climber, and a crafty liar. But even his enemies agreed that, for all his faults, Mesmer did believe in what he was doing, and that whatever it was he did—it worked. People took his treatments and they felt better.

Mesmer's theories about healing went through a gradual evolution and were never really consistent or original. In general he thought that the universe was permeated by an "aetheric continuum," or gas, which could be controlled by a force he called animal magnetism. By manipulating animal magnetism, the "magnetizer" could correct imbalance in the "continuum," which was the cause of all disease. It was a theory drawn primarily from astrology, alchemy and what was known of the physical sciences in the late eighteenth century.

According to Mesmer, control of animal magnetism was not merely a personal "gift"—it was something that could be taught or developed. Thus in addition to attracting the sick, he also attracted a crowd of wealthy disciples, who paid great sums to learn his technique. As was his custom, Mesmer quickly quarreled with all his disciples and many of them went on to form their own schools of magnetism.

Each disciple had his own individual ideas about how magnetism worked and what techniques should be used to control it. Mesmer himself started by actually putting magnets on the sick person's body, and he progressed to staring, hand waving and "magnetizing" various objects which were then supposed to have curative powers. The body of practice and theory that came to be called mesmerism or animal magnetism was very complicated, inconsistent, but astonishingly influential. The movement that grew from Mesmer's activities flourished under dozens of different names, spread throughout the Western world, and attracted some of the best minds of the late eighteenth and early nineteenth centuries to its banner. One may still find healers today who refer to themselves as "magnetists."

Mesmer is significant also because his methods were the first to be subjected to any sort of detailed scientific investigation. (Actually somewhat earlier von Hohenlohe was challenged by physicians to try to cure eighteen hospitalized patients. None showed any improvement.) Many physicians in France considered Mesmer not only a dangerous rival, but just plain dangerous. They persuaded the king to appoint a commission to study his claims and methods. Among those on the commission was Benjamin Franklin, then ambassador to France and a highly respected man in the field of science. The commission never was allowed to examine Mesmer's own work; he was, as I have said, a suspicious and uncooperative character. But they were able to make a detailed study of the work of one of Mesmer's close associates.

The commissioners concluded that they could find no trace of Mesmer's animal magnetism, but did say, "It is

FAITH HEALING

impossible not to admit that some great force acts upon and masters the patients." Since during the treatment patients went into violent convulsions, the investigators concluded that mesmerism was dangerous and should be banned. At that point Mesmer withdrew from France, and though he lived another thirty years was almost forgotten. Dangerous or not, the treatment made a lot of people feel better, and mesmerism or magnetism evolved into hypnotism and is still very much with us today.

Perhaps nothing shows the eternal and overpowering appeal of healing more clearly than the career of Mary Baker Eddy, although she would certainly reject the term healer. In 1862, Mary Baker Eddy (then Mary Baker Patterson) visited a healer named Phineas Parkhurst Quimby, who was staying at the International Hotel in Portland, Maine.

The forty-one-year-old woman had suffered all her life from a variety of unspecific, but debilitating ailments. Quimby treated her with a regimen which involved massage and hypnotism. Her cure was so spectacular that she went out and climbed up a monument just to prove her new-found strength. Until his death five years later, she was his passionate disciple and most enthusiastic propagandist. Thereafter she appropriated some of Quimby's ideas and all of the credit, and suppressed any mention of him in her works.

Mrs. Eddy went on to found Christian Science, which detractors always say is neither Christian nor scientific. Surely she was as controversial as anyone could possibly be. To her followers she was "Mother Mary," virtually the female Christ; to her critics she was a half-literate crank. Her basic point was that illness as an objective condition simply did not exist, that all illness was a manifestation of a mental state. In *Science and Health* she wrote, "You say a boil is painful—but that is impossible, for matter without mind is not painful. The boil simply manifests . . . a belief in pain, and this belief is called a boil."

It is easy enough to point out inconsistencies in Mary Baker Eddy's own career. She wore spectacles and had false teeth, and at least near the end of her long life used some drugs. It is a good deal less easy to explain the enormous success of Christian Science. With some justification Mary Baker Eddy has been called the greatest proselytizer since Mohammed.

In Mrs. Eddy's lifetime Christian Science grew from a congregation of one, the "discoverer" herself, to a major religion with millions of members, most of them middle-class and well-educated. Today Christian Science is a wealthy, well-established religion with thousands of centers primarily in the United States and Britain. These are run directly by the "Mother Church" in Boston. The *Christian Science Monitor* is one of the world's leading newspapers, the only newspaper published by a religious group to attain such status.

A network of Christian Science practitioners deal with illness of Church members and others. The Christian Science Church does not actually forbid its members to obtain medical treatment, especially in cases of broken bones or other ailments that may be treated without drugs. However, one cannot remain a good Christian Scientist and use medication of any kind.

The regular Christian Science meetings are not devoted to healing as such, but rather to reading from the Bible and from Mrs. Eddy's *Science and Health,* and to testimonies. But so much of this concerns health that it would be reasonable to conclude that Christian Science is a denomination devoted to promoting physical health by spiritual means.

Oddly, despite its extraordinarily controversial and zeal-

FAITH HEALING

ous beginnings, Christian Science leaders today appear to be worrying that their religion is losing its zeal and becoming too respectable. Many have speculated that membership is declining, and that what members remain are middle-aged or older. This is at least partly the result of a conscious church policy to play down the more exotic side of the religion. For example, Mrs. Eddy's *Science and Health* has been revised numerous times, and some of its stranger parts, like the ones about evil mesmerists causing so much trouble, have been eliminated or changed. But like other churches facing smothering respectability and attendant loss of interest, the Christian Science Church has been trying to prove that it, too, can still attract the young.

Comments Professor John B. Snook of the department of religion at Columbia University, "The Mother Church, not wanting to seem an institution of the middle-aged, has sponsored impressive rallies in recent years for young people, and it has filmed at least one such event to show that its message is still lively; but even this was obviously in respectable contrast to the rock music and drugs of young people who were called the 'Woodstock generation,' so that it is hard not to conclude that Christian Science has become a conventional institution hardly distinguishable in most respects from the conventional churches."

More of today is the Church of Scientology. Its founder, former science fiction writer L. Ron Hubbard, like Mrs. Eddy, is highly controversial. So are the doctrines and practices of the church. The main thrust of Scientology is that most disease is psychosomatic, and can be cured by scientological techniques. There have been repeated brushes with governmental authorities, both in the United States and in the other countries in which Scientology flourishes. Despite all this and despite numerous changes in doctrine by Hubbard, the Church of Scientology is an extremely viable institution. Whether it will, like Christian Science, be able to outlive its founder, no one can yet say. But today it claims several million followers worldwide, and the claim is probably not far wrong. In addition it attracts many young people, who one would think are less concerned about their health than the middle-aged members of Christian Science churches.

While both Christian Scientists and Scientologists might object to being classified under the heading faith healing, the label quite comfortably fits Oral Roberts, a man who until recently was America's number one faith healer. Roberts was a Pentecostal minister at the age of seventeen, and had himself attended many healing services. But he didn't discover his own healing powers until he was in his late twenties.

In many respects he practiced the conventional system of healing by laying on of hands and prayer, but since much of his work was carried on over radio and television, Roberts added a new wrinkle. He would ask his listeners and viewers to touch the loudspeaker or screen and be healed.

Roberts claimed many spectacular successes, but there were also a few well-publicized failures. During the 1960s it has been estimated that millions of dollars annually flowed through Roberts's organization, Healing Waters.

Over the last decade Oral Roberts appears to have succumbed to the lure of respectability. He has toned down his healing appeal, and begun to sound more like an orthodox evangelical preacher. He even became a Methodist minister, much to the horror of his old Pentecostal associates. He established his own university (Oral Roberts University in Tulsa, Oklahoma) which though only a few years old has managed to field championship-quality basketball teams. He is a rich man, and lives like one. Yet his basic appeal remains his reputation for healing powers.

With Oral Roberts now at least one step removed from faith healing, the title of America's number one faith healer would probably have to go to Pittsburgh's Kathryn Kuhlman (though she professes to hate the term). Kathryn Kuhlman has been a healer since she was in her teens, and she is now nearing seventy. Miss Kuhlman also works by touch and prayer and her syndicated television show reaches a wide audience. Her sermons or talks are so filled with overpowering sweetness, and delivered with such a show of emotion, that a nonbeliever is quite likely to gag at them. But to the hundreds of thousands, and perhaps millions, who feel that they personally have somehow been helped by Kathryn Kuhlman, she is a miracle worker.

Despite her highly theatrical presentation, Miss Kuhlman does radiate sincerity. She is humble concerning her gifts. Beyond insisting that the healing power comes from God, she has no elaborate theories. She is also genuinely upset by failure, which she acknowledges does happen in some cases.

Although America's most famous healers are fundamentalist Christians, Harry Edwards, Britain's most famous healer (who also has a considerable following in the United States), is an ardent spiritualist. The octogenarian Edwards has a "sanctuary" at Shere, Surrey, which is very nearly as famous as Lourdes as a place of healing. But one does not need to visit Harry Edwards in person in order to be healed. Some 600,000 letters requesting aid pass through his office every year.

Edwards says that his cures are accomplished through the agency of the spirits of the dead, who because of their superhuman knowledge and powers are able to cure many, though not all diseases. Faith on the part of the patient is unnecessary in Edwards' scheme of things. He offers the name of the sufferer to the spirits, who will then either cure the disease or give a diagnosis of it. Edwards acknowledges failures, though he is at a loss to explain them. He does not contend, however, that even the spirits can raise the dead or reverse aging. Edwards suggests that there are certain spiritual laws in the universe that neither the spirits nor God Himself will upset.

Few modern-day healers will claim to rival the feat of the raising of Lazarus, though a number of cult leaders, even in fairly recent times, have claimed that they could do this, or that they themselves would rise from the dead. There are several sad-funny stories of cultists standing a vigil over the corpse of their departed leader confidently expecting him to rise, until the health department came in and hauled away the decaying cadaver as a public nuisance. One cultist had a tape recording of his own voice predicting his own resurrection played at his funeral. Another had to abandon plans to raise the dead when he became concerned that the faithful were about to start shipping corpses to him.

Mention must be made here of Edgar Cayce, if only because he is so well-known today. Cayce wasn't really a typical faith healer (if there really is such a thing). He was more of a medical clairvoyant. He would go into a trance and diagnose the disease of someone who might be miles away. He would also often suggest treatments, generally drawn from homeopathic or chiropractic lore. His fame today rests not so much on his medical diagnosis, but on the fact that while entranced he would issue all manner of prophecies. However, during his lifetime Cayce was most famous for his medical pronouncements. Today those who are followers of the Cayce cult claim that on the basis of their extensive records they can prove that Cayce cures had a success rate of somewhere around 80 percent.

It is really quite impossible to estimate how many faith or paranormal healers are operating in the world today. Much depends on how one wishes to define "faith healer." One authority has estimated that at the present time there are "probably well over ten thousand psychic healers" in England alone. In America, if one includes all the Christian Science practitioners and the Pentecostal or Holiness preachers for whom healing is a regular part of the service, the number must be far, far higher. Many modern witches or followers of other exotic religions also claim healing powers.

The 80 percent rate of cure claimed for Cayce is on the order of that claimed by most other modern-day healers. How do they do it? More basically, do they do it at all?

For a phenomenon as widespread, well-publicized, and important, if only because so many are involved in it, there has been astonishingly little scientific study of faith healing. Part of the problem lies with the healers who resist scientific scrutiny because they fear it or feel that it is somehow degrading to have their powers doubted. "God does not operate in a test tube" was how one healer explained his refusal to cooperate with an investigation. Another serious problem is created by the attitudes of scientific and medical researchers who often consider faith healing is a subject unworthy of study or too difficult to be studied in a worthwhile manner.

The problems faced by anyone wishing to examine the subject of faith healing are formidable. Do healers "cure" people? What is meant by "cure" in the first place? In the old days there was little doubt. St. Beuno, a Welsh saint of the seventh century, was said to have "cured" a girl named Winefride, whose head had been chopped off by her angry lover. The saint merely replaced the head in its former position, where it re-grew, leaving only a slight scar. There is no ambiguity about such incidents—either they happened or they didn't. There are plenty of similar tales from ancient days or distant places, but no modern faith healer has claimed he successfully replaced a severed head, or even, as far as can be determined, a severed finger. Even cases in which faith cures are supposed to have worked on any traumatic injury are surprisingly rare.

There are plenty of claims that healers have cured various "incurable" ailments, but when is an ailment "incurable"? A person at the point of death from terminal cancer, or whose life can be sustained only by a heart-lung machine because his heart will no longer function, can truly be said to be incurable. But faith cures in such cases are as rare as cures of severed heads.

Who determines that a disease is "incurable"—a physician? Incorrect diagnosis is not unheard of. Sometimes a physician will pronounce a disease as incurable merely because he is unable to cure it—but that is not the same thing as being incurable. Doctors can, and often do, disagree. There are many examples of "incurable" diseases that were cured by a new course of treatment.

In the records of faith cures it often appears as though the patient himself pronounces his disease to be incurable. After going from physician to physician without finding any relief, he goes to a faith healer. If he does feel better after a few sessions with the healer, he is naturally going to think that his previously "incurable" disease has been cured by something that the healer did.

A further problem is raised by what is known to physicians as spontaneous remission. Sometimes, diseases thought to be incurable by medical authorities cure themselves, though no one knows why. It is estimated that in somewhere between one in 10,000 and one in 100,000 cases of cancer diagnosed as terminal, pain ceases, damage to tissue stops, and cancers shrink and sometimes even disappear. Doctors suspect that such spontaneous remissions have something to do with the body's immune system, but why it works in a few cases and not in the vast majority or why the cancer took so long to trigger an immune reaction, no one knows. In any event, spontaneous remission, not only of cancer but of other diseases, is a well-known, though admittedly rare, medical phenomenon. It has taken place in cases where doctors had ceased medical treatments, and where the patient had received no form of unorthodox treatment like faith healing.

If a patient in whom a spontaneous remission had taken place had also happened to visit a faith healer, then the cure would doubtless be attributed to the healer, who could claim another "miracle" cure.

Critics of faith healing say that when it works, it works only on diseases that are functional, hysterical or psychosomatic. The terms all mean roughly the same thing, the point being that the diseases are mental or emotional rather than organic in origin. Such ailments are often unkindly and unfairly called "imaginary," as though the patient were some sort of weakling or fake who, by an exercise of "will," would be able to shake off the affliction. But the pain and disability of such "imaginary" ailments are quite real. A person suffering from hysterical paralysis of the legs can't walk any more than the person who has suffered a spinal injury can. The cause of the paralysis is different, the treatment may be different, but both sufferers are unable to walk.

There is little doubt that healers have had greater success at treating functional ailments than organic ones, as most healers themselves would probably agree. In Mesmer's time many of the cures were apparently performed upon people (usually women) who had become blind or paralyzed for no apparent reason. A century and a quarter later Sigmund

Freud and his followers were able to successfully treat many of the same symptoms through psychoanalysis, though Freud clearly recognized the psychological origins of the affliction.

Today conditions that once were labeled hysterical paralysis or hysterical blindness appear to be a good deal less common than they were in the past. No one really knows why, but it does appear that patterns of the symptoms of mental disturbance change, just as other disease patterns change. This does not mean that psychologically created ailments have declined, merely that they are different.

There is a good deal of controversy over which diseases are functional and which organic. Diseases as diverse as cancer and asthma have been labeled by some as largely psychosomatic. It may be that we have not yet been able to discover the organic cause of such diseases, and psychosomatic is a term that covers a lot of territory. Besides, many people resent being told that they have a psychosomatic condition, because it appears to imply that they are somehow "crazy."

The spectacular success that conventional medicine has had against many organic diseases over the last few hundred years led many physicians to ignore, or drastically downplay, the mental component of disease. Today, however, the balance has swung back, at least somewhat. British psychiatrist Dr. D. J. West, who conducted some important studies of faith healing, says that "psychological influence plays some part in almost all illnesses and a large part in many."

But which illness, and how large a part? That is a problem which confronts anyone who attempts to study the subject of faith healing. Here there is no agreement. Doctors believe, but do not know for sure, that psychological stress plays an important part in the development of heart disease. Responsible people have estimated that one case of cancer in three is caused by unhappiness. Though most medical scientists would disagree strongly with this estimate, Sir Heneage Ogilvie, a distinguished British surgeon, has stated flatly that "the happy man never gets cancer."

Moreover, a lot of unhappy people get symptoms—painful, serious and often crippling symptoms—that send them rushing to doctors for aid. It has been estimated that anywhere from one third to one half of the visits to doctors in America today are made by patients suffering from nonorganic diseases. Once again we must stress that these illnesses are not "imaginary" in the sense that the patient is "making them up" or has any conscious control over them.

Our mind has more control over "involuntary" bodily functions than we once thought possible. The reverse side of this coin is that our mind can also cause disorders in our bodily functions and detectable alterations in physical conditions. Psychological stress seems to lower the body's resistance and make it more prone to organic diseases. Stress may raise the blood pressure, which may ultimately result in damage to the kidneys and heart. There is nothing "imaginary" or "crazy" about any of this.

Admitting, then, that psychological conditions can create or exacerbate disease, is the opposite also true? Can these conditions be reversed or cured by psychological methods? Practically everyone will admit they can to a degree.

For centuries physicians have recognized that a good "bedside manner" is helpful with practically any disease. This "bedside manner" generally consists of equal parts of confidence and sympathetic understanding. Studies of hospitalized patients have shown that those who are visited regularly by physicians tend to recover more quickly than those who are not. The reason is not necessarily that the physician prescribes any special treatment when he visits, but rather that the patient feels that somebody cares and is "doing something." Physicians also know that they have to be extremely careful about what they say to their patients, for a careless word, a hint of despair or hopelessness, may send the patient careening into a relapse. In the second century A.D. the Roman physician Galen wrote, "He cures most in whom most are confident."

The placebo effect remains one of the most persistent, puzzling and powerful phenomena in medicine. The placebo, a word which means "I please you," is most familiarly a capsule or pill containing sugar or some other nontherapeutic ingredient, or a bottle of impressively colored water. It can be quite literally the cure for which there is no disease, but which may help in the treatment of all diseases. Practically any treatment regimen can act as a placebo. Even operations which were later found to be useless still helped some patients, because the patient thought they were supposed to help.

For centuries, bleeding and purging were common treatments for practically every disease. It is now said that patients recovered in spite of, not because of, these treatments, for not only were they useless, but they actually weakened the patient. And yet it is hard to escape the conclusion that even such drastic and dangerous methods also had a placebo effect.

The important thing is that the patient believe that what he is drinking, injecting or doing is going to help him. The key element therefore is faith. It helps immeasurably if the doctor also has faith, for then his confidence reinforces that of the patient.

A standard method of testing a new drug, or in fact any new treatment, is the double blind test. Half the patients in the test are given the new drug, the other half are given an

FAITH HEALING

inert substance made to look exactly like the drug. If the drug is contained in a pink pill, the placebo is also a pink pill. The test is more accurate when even the doctors administering the substances don't know which is which, otherwise their attitudes might affect the subjects. If the physicians have to evaluate the treatment knowing which is which, it might color their evaluation of success or failure. Very often it has been found that a placebo works just as well, or just as poorly, as the drug. Some subjects develop rashes, headaches or other side effects from injections of colored water.

It has been suggested that many of the drugs currently in use, particularly nonprescription, over-the-counter drugs, also depend primarily on the placebo effect. There has been a good deal of agitation of late to make sure that drugs are not only harmless, but also effective. As a result drug companies have been hard-pressed to show that some of their more popular items have any beneficial organic effect whatsoever, and some have been withdrawn from the market. Repeated clinical studies have shown that a sugar pill will work as well as the most powerful pain killer for about one third of all patients.

Writing in the magazine *Psychology Today,* physiologist Frederick J. Evans observed: "An important clue to how the placebo works came from the observations of Henry Beecher on the Anzio beachhead during World War II. Of the soldiers who suffered grievous but not fatal wounds, only about one third wanted medication to relieve their pain. Two thirds refused the medication (but they complained bitterly about the discomfort experienced if an inept corpsman failed to make a successful venous puncture). According to Beecher, the wounded soldier experienced relief, thankfulness to escape alive from the battlefield, and even euphoria. The soldiers' wounds meant that they would be removed from combat. They no longer needed to fear danger. In contrast, Beecher later observed patients with similar wounds in a civilian hospital who demanded and consumed large quantities of pain-killing drugs. The civilian patients needed drugs to relieve the unbearable suffering as they worried about the consequences of their injuries." Evans suggests that placebos become "a standard item in the physician's black bag."

Most physicians assume that the placebo effect has something to do with suggestion. We do know that suggestion alone can produce dramatic physical effects, as in deep hypnosis. Individuals become insensitive to pain and are able to do things physically that they would be incapable of doing in a normal state. It is also known that suggestion does not operate only during hypnotic trances, but that it can be effective in normal waking states. A spellbinding orator does not put his audience into a hypnotic trance, but his words can produce measurable alterations in bodily functions, and can profoundly influence behavior.

We are all subject to a delicately balanced and poorly understood interaction of physical and mental influences. Recognition of this fact enormously complicates any attempt to evaluate the claims made for faith healing of any sort.

Most proponents of faith healing would admit that the placebo effect or suggestion does play a part in the success of many healers. They do tend to stress, however, that cures have been performed on people who were skeptical of the healer's powers. It is difficult, of course, to decide if a person is truly skeptical. If he didn't believe in the healer, why did he go to him in the first place? Perhaps a core of belief lay beneath a crust of skepticism. Even a skeptic faced with a serious illness may be ready to believe anything. In-depth psychological interviews of individuals before they went to faith healers might help to cast some light on this problem, but such information simply does not exist.

Supporters of faith healing also counter with the argument, What's wrong with suggestion if it works? The answer is nothing is wrong with suggestion. If the healer is able to alleviate suffering and even cure diseases by suggestion alone, that's fine. But it isn't what most people mean when they say faith healing. If the healer has no more power at his command than does a doctor with a sugar pill, or a complete charlatan with a good delivery, then it is the patient rather than the healer who should be of interest.

Faith healing implies the action of powers beyond the normal powers of the mind. But since we are not sure what the limits of the "normal" powers of the mind are in relation to the body, or even what powers are "normal," we are presented with some rather tricky problems. Still to conclude that faith healing really exists, it is fair to require that something beyond suggestion is operating.

While suggestion and the placebo effect present the biggest tangle in the study of faith healing, there are others. Many people who seek out the services of a faith healer are, at the same time, undergoing medical treatment of some sort. If the patient gets better, how can we be sure that it was the healer and not the orthodox treatment that caused the improvement?

Medical oddities may also account for a small number of faith cures, but these could be spectacular. There is, for example, a phenomenon known as "cure by biopsy." A tissue sample is removed from a patient suspected of having cancer. When the tissue is examined, it is found to be cancerous, but unknown to the doctors, the sample removed contained all the cancerous tissue in the patient's body. On further examination it is discovered that the cancer has "disappeared." This doesn't happen very often, but it does happen. If such an individual, after getting a diagnosis of cancer, then went to a faith healer, he would automatically assume that the faith healer cured him.

Some faith healers employ little tricks which work surprisingly well. One that was widely used in healing revivals throughout the rural South and Midwest was a cure for deafness. A common cause of hearing impairment is a buildup of wax in the ear. This is quickly apparent to a doctor, but the rural poor often do not see doctors regularly, though they may go to faith healers. As the person suffering from hearing impairment goes up to the platform, the healer "lays hands" on his ears. Actually he claps his hands hard over the ears, and the impact may loosen the wax plug and produce a "miraculous" improvement in hearing.

Some headaches and back pains can be cured or alleviated by spinal manipulation. Often healers who use a vigorous laying on of hands look suspiciously like they are practicing some sort of manipulation, and the subject might be just as well off going to a chiropractor.

Another problem involves a definition of the word cure. Is a patient cured when all his symptoms disappear? Or most of them? And for how long? Can a patient be considered cured only when an examination reveals no trace of the disease from which he was suffering, or is a patient cured if he simply feels better? There are a number of tragic cases on record where patients pronounced themselves "cured" of a disease after visiting a faith healer, only to die of that very same disease a few weeks or months later.

Practically every disease has its ups and downs, and patients have their good days and their bad ones. The psychological lift given by a visit to a healer may help the patient have a good period. During such a time the patient's relatives, friends and even the patient himself have a tendency to say that he has been "cured." Such sentiments may be born more from hope than belief. There is a short-lived euphoria, but afterwards the old symptoms return. Followup studies are vital in the evaluation of any medical treatment, and hopeful initial results are often reversed by finding that the symptoms have returned and the disease never really went away.

Interestingly, accounts of "successful" faith cures often contain the postscript that the patient either died or returned to his or her former state of illness a few months or years later. Some healers appear to consider any improvement a "cure." While any alleviation of suffering or prolongation of life is to be welcomed, it is not the same thing as a cure. The distinction should be made clear, but often it isn't.

One must also realize that at least a small percentage of the claims made for healers are either entirely false or at wide variance with the facts of the case.

All of these interlocking factors must be taken into account in any evaluation of faith healing. In judging the success or failure of even the simplest of orthodox medical treatments, an enormous amount of record keeping is involved. The same sort of record keeping would be necessary for a scientific evaluation of faith healing. But despite claims by faith healers that they have elaborate "scientific" documentation for their cures, such records do not, in fact, exist.

Many healers and their supporters seem to believe, that simply because something is written down it constitutes "documentary proof." What are commonly presented as "proof" are testimonials from individuals who believed that the healer helped them. Most of these are doubtless honest and sincere, but they should in no way be confused with the type of painstaking fact gathering considered absolutely necessary for most medical studies, or even with a well-kept medical case history. Too often "documentary proof" comes down to little more than letters of gratitude or newspaper clippings. A century ago, any patent medicine seller, any traveling snake oil dealer could come up with the same sort of "evidence." Even today, the testimonial is a widely used advertising gimmick.

Most healers have neither the time, money nor inclination to carry out the kind of research that would be necessary if their claims are ever to become scientifically respectable. The letters of thanks, or the apparently happy people walking away from the platform after a healing service, are enough for them. "Why bother with record keeping," they say, "when you can see with your own eyes a man throw away his cane and walk upright for the first time in ten years?"

But that isn't enough, not if the subject is to be treated seriously by intelligent people. The study of faith healing today is at about the stage that the study of extrasensory perception was nearly a century ago. We are still engaged in the equivalent of collecting ghost stories. There is a good deal of interesting and suggestive anecdotal evidence. The subject itself is potentially of great importance. Yet the conclusive evidence is lacking, and there seems to be a real reluctance on the part of faith healers and their supporters to try to go out and get that conclusive evidence.

Many of the healers say that the proof is already there, and no more is necessary. Others believe that the subject itself, because of its basically spiritual nature, is really beyond the realm of scientific investigation. Still others feel (with considerable justification) that scientists are already prejudiced against the practice of faith healing, and would not acknowledge proof even if it were presented to them. Scientific interference, they contend, would disturb the healing process. And indeed some may fear that faith healing can be ex-

FAITH HEALING

plained in ordinary terms, and they would thus find themselves without the phenomenon to which they had devoted most of their lives. But still the attempt must be made, just as it was made (and is still being made) in the area of extrasensory perception. It will not make much difference to most of us if someone finally proves that the Loch Ness monster exists. It will make a great deal of difference if we prove faith healing is real.

The best documentation of faith cures are kept by the Roman Catholic Church in connection with the great healing shrine at Lourdes. Lourdes is a small town in the Pyrenees where on February 11, 1858, fourteen-year-old Bernadette Soubirous reported the first of a series of visions of the Virgin. The account attracted an enormous amount of attention. Bernadette was subsequently canonized, and Lourdes became a place of pilgrimage.

Interestingly enough, in the visions reported by Bernadette, the Virgin made no specific claims of healing for those who worshiped at her shrine or bathed in the spring which marks the site of her appearance. But as often happens, a place that has a reputation for a miraculous event also gains a reputation as a healing shrine. Healing and holiness are closely linked in the public mind.

By the 1890s, "miracle" cures were being reported regularly from Lourdes, and a tremendous controversy had grown up. The authenticity of these cures was both passionately defended and sharply criticized in the press. The healing reputation of Lourdes was given a great boost in 1903 when Alexis Carrel, a Nobel prize winner in medicine, confirmed a number of "miraculous" cures.

As early as 1882 an organization called *Bureau des Constatations Medicales,* staffed by Roman Catholic physicians, was set up to examine the thousands of claims of cures that are made for Lourdes every year. The organization set quite strict standards for authenticating cures. Among the rules are that the sufferer must have been certified by expert diagnosis to have a serious organic condition that was either untreatable, or amenable only to lengthy treatment. The cure must be both immediate and long-lasting. The British Society for Psychical Research also examined the claims made for Lourdes, in 1884, but there were no firm conclusions contained in the final SPR report.

The fame of Lourdes has grown, and travel has become easier, so that now millions visit the shrine every year. And yet, in the nearly one hundred years of its existence the *Bureau des Constatations,* has approved only a thousand or so cures as being acceptable on medical grounds. The number of cures authenticated every year has not risen though the number of visitors has. The *Bureau* also has a strict set of theological standards it applies to accounts of cures. When these are taken into account, only about fifty cures have been sanctioned in the entire history of the shrine.

Using only the medical standards, that means that about one in two million who visit Lourdes are "cured." And even when the *Bureau* standards for cures are ignored, it has been estimated that a mere 2 percent of those who visit Lourdes report any marked physical improvement at all. Roman Catholics assert that the majority of those who visit Lourdes today do not expect a physical cure so much as a spiritual uplift, and that the shrine is primarily religious and not medical. Nor is belief in the efficacy of the shrine an article of faith for Catholics.

But no matter how tiny the number of cures, if they were truly miraculous, this would be highly significant. So how good is the *Bureau's* authentication? Dr. D. J. West examined eleven recent "established" Lourdes miracles and found

FAITH HEALING

what he considered to be serious flaws in the records for every one of them. There was not a single clear "miracle" of the type in which St. Beuno successfully replaced a girl's severed head. The cures generally concerned things like malignant tumors, in which spontaneous remission of the disease is always a possibility. In several cases of tuberculosis cures West felt that the presence of the disease had not been sufficiently established in the first place. He was also generally critical of the *Bureau's* clinical facilities and its record keeping. Finally West wondered why it was that elderly spinsters appeared to receive benefits from Lourdes far in excess of any other group in the population. The case for the miraculous powers of this most famous, and most closely examined, of all healing shrines remains unproven to the bulk of the scientific and medical community.

Another British psychiatrist, Dr. Louis Rose, tried a different approach to the subject of faith healing. Rose had been interested in faith healing for many years, but was constantly frustrated by the elusive nature of the evidence. He tried to arrange control experiments in which healers like Harry Edwards would treat hospitalized patients whose conditions had been certified by competent medical authorities. But neither the healers nor the hospitals were particularly anxious to cooperate, and the project never got off the ground.

Dr. Rose then determined to try to collect all the accounts of faith cures that he could find, select the best of them and follow them through by contacting the patients, their doctors and anyone else who could shed light on the case. His aim was not to find out if healers made a significant percentage of their patients feel better, but to locate even one single case in which the intervention of the healer produced miraculous results. Dr. Rose stated quite frankly that it was not his purpose to find out how faith healing worked, but if it worked at all. This outlook rather upset some British psychical researchers, who tend to consider healing an "established fact," but they cooperated in the project anyway.

Appeals for accounts of cures were printed in psychic and religious publications as well as in medical journals. Prominent healers were contacted and asked to submit their best cases. Dr. Rose described his task as "a painstaking, sometimes tedious, sometimes frustrating but always, I believed, worth-while process." The results of two years of inquiry were reported first in a lecture to the Society for Psychical Research, and then printed in the *British Medical Journal* in December 1954.

Of the 95 good cases brought to Dr. Rose's attention, he was unable to obtain confirming records for 58 of them. In another 22 there was so great a variation between the claims made for the cure and the available records, that further investigation seemed pointless. Typical of these was a case reported in the newspapers in which a boy, supposedly paralyzed and unable to speak since birth, had been cured after doctors had pronounced him as hopelessly incurable. The boy's medical records showed that he had been hospitalized for several serious infectious diseases, for which he had been satisfactorily treated, but there was no indication that he had ever been paralyzed or unable to speak at any time during his life.

Of the remaining fifteen cases there was one in which the patient continued to deteriorate after receiving treatment from the healer, three cases in which there was some temporary improvement followed by a relapse, four in which there was definite improvement but in which the patient was also receiving orthodox medical treatment while going to a faith healer. On the more positive side, there were four cases in which the patient felt much better and was able to function

FAITH HEALING

more normally after treatment by the healer, although doctors could find no objective improvement in the condition. In two other cases, Dr. Rose concluded that there was a possibility that the healer contributed to the amelioration of an organic condition.

Finally there was a single case in which a definite organic disability appeared to have been cured after treatment by a healer. This was a case in which a physician said that he had been cured of severe back pains, and later of a small hernia, by faith healing. Dr. Rose, however, suggested that the back pains may have been due to what is commonly called a "slipped disc." This is a condition in which attacks of pain are severe, but unpredictable, often disappearing for years for no known reason. This can happen with or without the intervention of a healer.

The hernia was not so easy to explain away. Wrote Dr. Rose, "The matter of the hernia would at first sight seem to afford incontrovertible evidence in favor of the healer. However, this phenomenon of spontaneous cure is known by surgeons to occur in the absence of therapeutic intervention."

From his study, Dr. Rose concluded that "whatever else I might have discovered, I had not come within hailing distance of a single example of the type of 'miracle cure' which I was seeking."

Since that time Dr. Rose has attempted to follow up on all the promising accounts of cures brought to his attention. The information, as before, remains elusive and frustrating. The miracle cure performed by St. Beuno remained as far away as ever.

Summing up his years of continuing investigation in his book *Faith Healing* (revised edition published 1971), Dr. Rose said that for the existence of a special and unique phenomenon that might be labeled "faith healing" he could find only "shadowy claims and cases which refuse to assume substance."

"Yet," he continued, "the shadow remains a massive one, and I certainly do not feel that I have reached the end of a road."

A somewhat different approach to the subject of faith healing has received a good deal of publicity in the last few years. This approach did not grow from the claims of the healers themselves, but rather from what might be termed "unorthodox botany." There has been a good deal of speculation that people who talked to their plants, and loved their plants, got them to grow better than people who treated them as—well—plants, and confined their attention to watering and occasionally adding a bit of plant food.

The next step was to try to test this approach into the laboratory. In several experiments a group of identical potted plants was divided into two parts. One group was "loved," the other merely "cared for," and the "loved" plants grew better. Even more dramatic results seemed to be obtained when one group of plants was "prayed over."

One theory that grew out of these observations was that neither the praying nor the talking was what caused the plants to grow, but rather that certain people emitted some sort of unknown radiation that was in some way beneficial to plants.

An individual who had attracted some attention in this regard was Oskar Estebany, a former Hungarian Army colonel. Estebany was tested by Dr. Bernard Grad of McGill University, Montreal. According to Grad's reports, plants watered with a solution touched by Estebany grew significantly better than plants that were watered with an identical solution which Estebany had not touched.

FAITH HEALING

If this unknown radiation worked on plants, why not on animals, so Estebany's healing powers were tested. A group of mice were given identical wounds. The group was then divided into three parts. The first group was allowed to heal without any additional treatment. The second group was given heat treatments, which are believed to promote healing. The third group was given to Estebany. He did not actually touch the mice, but only handled their cages. Still it appeared as if this group healed more quickly than those treated with heat or left untreated. It was also reported that Estebany could retard the growth of goiters produced in mice by iodine-deficient diets and hasten their disappearance when the mice were returned to a normal diet.

Reports of a similar nature have appeared from time to time in the popular press and in journals, primarily those of psychical research and parapsychology organizations. They sound sensational and conclusive to the general public, but they are far from that. There are many reasons why one group of mice may heal more quickly than another that have nothing whatever to do with unknown radiation. One possibility is a subtle difference in the way one of the groups is treated during the healing period. If, for example, the experimenters were out to prove the reality of healing, which they almost certainly were, they might, without meaning to, be more attentive to the group of mice handled by the healer.

Still another possibility for error rests in the way in which the conclusions were drawn. The difference in healing between the three groups was not all that great. Perhaps in evaluating the healing process, the experimenters were influenced by their own bias toward the radiation explanation. Similar errors have been made so often in the past that they are almost routine.

There is no proof that the wrong conclusions were drawn

from the Estebany experiment. But it can't be considered conclusive until a great deal more work is done in this field. Though the layman is usually unaware of this, each year there are hundreds of scientific experiments performed in which the results appear to contradict widely held theories. This is particularly true in medical research. Very often these results are brought about because of some fault in the experimental design or implementation. Extreme caution is necessary in cases like this, but alas, since faith healing is a subject which touches so many so deeply, caution is usually the first casualty.

Even if it ultimately turns out that the faith healer controls no special powers, that his undoubted ability to make some sick people feel better is the result of suggestion alone, all the interest in the subject still will have had a beneficial effect. It has helped to remind orthodox medical practitioners that a patient is a human being with a mind as well as a body. It is less possible now than ever before to know just where the "body" leaves off and the "mind" begins. Just because the healer may not be able to produce the "miracles" he claims for his treatment does not mean that he is not doing anything worthwhile, and it does not mean that medicine has nothing to learn from faith healing.

Whether the claims of faith healing are finally substantiated by careful investigation or not, the practice will undoubtedly continue to appeal to millions, even in places where advanced medical treatment is available, just as it always has throughout history. So long as there is suffering, faith healing will continue to exist. For this reason alone it should be treated more seriously by the scientific community than it has in the past.

5
EXTRASENSORY DREAMING

THERE is a persistent rumor that the United States government is sponsoring some sort of "secret" research into extrasensory perception. I have often been asked about these "secret" projects. When I say that I don't know anything about them and doubt that they exist at all, the response is often a knowing wink meaning, "Come on, you can't fool me" or a sympathetic nod meaning, "So they've put one over on you too."

But the fact is that I don't know of any "secret" research, nor have I heard or seen any plausible evidence to indicate that such research is taking place now or has in the past. Of course, if the project were truly secret I wouldn't know about it, but neither, I suspect, would all of those who claim to have inside knowledge.

In truth, the United States government, like any other large bureaucracy, tends to be extremely conservative about giving large sums of money for any offbeat projects. There are no ESP lobbies, no congressmen whose districts depend heavily on ESP for their prosperity. While there are a number of congressmen, both senators and representatives, who are deeply interested in psychic subjects, and a certain number of research scientists connected with the government who are also interested in the possibility of research in these areas, this interest has never been translated into dollars. Not until recently, that is.

Perhaps it is an indication of the growing scientific respectability of ESP, or just of the growing popular interest in the subject that the United States government finally has made a grant, and not a secret one either, for the study of extrasensory perception.

The grant given through the National Institute of Mental Health was $52,000, a modest amount as such things go, but significant because it is the first major federal grant awarded for parapsychological research. The grant was given to Maimonides Medical Center in Brooklyn, which has been carrying on research in extrasensory perception in dreams for over a decade. The pioneers of this research at Maimonides are Drs. Montague Ullman and Stanley Krippner.

The work at Maimonides has been called "the space program of parapsychology." The title has been given not merely because of the pioneering nature of the research, but because even before the federal grant, the Maimonides experiments had been exceptionally well-funded. (Though like all researchers, they complain bitterly, and with considerable justification, that they are chronically short of funds.) Most parapsychologists have trouble getting enough money to buy a new pack of ESP cards. The Maimonides laboratory has been able to afford a mass of sophisticated and expensive equipment. As a result the researchers there have opened whole new areas of investigation and have tested well over 100 subjects over extended periods. The Maimonides dream laboratory research is to parapsychology of the 1970s what Dr. J. B. Rhine's card guessing experiments were in the 1930s.

EXTRASENSORY DREAMING

The idea that some form of extrasensory perception might take place while dreaming is hardly an original one. Dreaming is the oldest, best-known, and most universal "altered state of consciousness." Most people have believed strongly that the contents of dreams were highly significant. To some, sleep was the time when God or the gods or spirits of the dead were able to communicate with the living through the medium of dreams. Others believed that at night the soul or spirit left the body and wandered throughout the world and the universe, conversed with other spirits and with God. Dreams were supposed to be memories of these travels and conversations.

Whatever the explanation given for dreams, people took them very seriously. The proper interpretation of dreams, for dreams are rarely straightforward, was a highly valued skill. The ancient Hebrews, who scorned the astrology and the other complicated divination methods practiced by their neighbors, treated dreams and dream interpretation with reverence. To the Hebrews a dream was nothing less than a message from God.

The Greeks, who were great systematizers, worked out extraordinarily complicated rules for dream interpretation. The rules were so complicated that they provided little help for dream interpreters. The Romans, who could be skeptical about many spiritual matters, still thought that dreams might provide a key to the future. During Christian times we hear less of the importance of dreams, at least officially. Revelations from God were supposed to come through his Church, and individual inspiration was generally discouraged. Saints might have visions or prophetic dreams, but more ordinary folk were assumed to be either tormented or misled by demons in their dreams. Still the belief that dreaming provided a special view of reality, either present or future, remained strong, and throughout the Middle Ages there continued to be a lively, if somewhat underground, business in dream interpretation.

In addition to being prophetic, dreams also got the reputation of being a time at which hidden creative energies were unleashed. Friedrich Kekulé, a nineteenth-century German scientist, puzzling over the chemical structure of benzene, reported dreaming of a snake eating its tail, and awakening with the inspiration that the structure of benzene was a ring. The poet Samuel Taylor Coleridge said that the poem "Kubla Khan" came to him in a dream. There are numerous other examples from history. What it all adds up to is that most of us regard dreaming as something rather special.

Perhaps the most influential recent reinterpretation of the meaning of dreams was made around the year 1900 by the Viennese neurologist Sigmund Freud. Freud contended that the content of dreams comes from inside the dreamer rather than from any God-given glimpse of external realities. Dreams, said Freud, were drawn from the life of the dreamer —indeed, often from events that had taken place in the day preceding the dream. But they might also contain symbolic, obscure and veiled accounts of various fears, desires and anxieties, mostly sexual in nature. Dreams in Freud's view could provide the key to unlocking buried fragments of the dreamer's early life, which might be the cause of neurosis.

But Freud's theories, and in fact all the older beliefs about dreams, were based on morning-after reports by the dreamers. The dreamers themselves generally realized that dreams that had seemed vivid and clear at the moment of awakening slipped quickly from memory sometimes in just a few minutes, and that in retelling a dream, many details are lost or altered.

Even leaving aside the meaning of dreams, there were a number of unanswered but intriguing questions about the subject. Why was it that some people seemed to dream frequently, and others rarely if at all? Or why were some periods of a person's life rich in dreams and others barren? Were dreams instantaneous, or did they happen in real time—that is, did the dream take as long as the actions performed in the dream should have? Did most people dream in black and white and have dreams in color only when they contained a highly charged emotional content? Was the dreamer cut off from external or visceral happenings, or did such things as the ringing of an alarm or indigestion somehow become incorporated into his dreams?

All of these questions and a lot more about dreaming were answered in the late 1950s and early 1960s, when scientists, aided by such machines as the EEG and other physical monitoring equipment, were able to make the first objective exploration of the previously unknown one third of our life that we spend asleep. The story is too well-known to bear repeating in any detail. For our purposes we need only summarize a few of the major findings.

The most surprising finding was that all of us dream every night. On an average, 20 percent of each night's sleep is spent dreaming. The difference is not that some people dream a great deal and others rarely dream, it is rather that some people recall their dreams better than others. Dreams do take place in real time, are almost always in color, and they can be affected by external stimulus or internal sensations.

In addition, dreams were found to be necessary to our health and well being. If a person keeps having his dreams interrupted, and is thus deprived of normal dream time, he will be very irritable in the morning. The following night he will spend more than the usual amount of time dreaming. If dream deprivation is continued over an extended period, an individual will begin to display signs of acute mental disorientation. These symptoms can be dispelled only if he is allowed to "make up" his dreams.

Some substances like alcohol tend to suppress dreams. This may be one of the reasons that we feel so rotten after a night of drinking. It has been suggested that delirium tremens, the hallucinations including the famous little pink elephants that often afflict alcoholics, are really dreams that have been forced into waking consciousness after a long period of deprivation due to drinking. Other hallucinations and visions may also be forms of waking dreams.

The dream studies also confirmed the suspicion that we do not remember our dreams very well. By checking their instruments, researchers could tell exactly when one of their subjects was in the midst of a dream. They could awaken him then, or as soon as the dream had ended, and have him record his recollections immediately. The same dream might be forgotten completely by the following morning, or it might be recalled quite differently.

It turned out that all the fancy theories about the "meaning" of dreams had been based on partial and unreliable evidence.

Well then, what did dreams mean? The dream research that was being conducted at a dozen or more sleep and dream laboratories throughout the country was not primarily aimed at interpreting the content of dreams, though in nearly twenty years of research the laboratories have accumulated an enormous number of dream records.

Many dreams are quite straightforward—"I dreamed I had to go to the bathroom and when I woke up, you know what? I had to go to the bathroom." A lot of dream time seems to be involved with anxiety or frustration—dreaming about waiting for buses that never arrive, trying to reach a door that always is just beyond reach. One severely depressed

EXTRASENSORY DREAMING

person reported a recurring dream of standing in front of a Coke machine that delivered only the syrup, no fizz. For many people it appears that their dream life is not notably happier than their waking life, and may in fact be worse. As often as not the incidents in the dreams are drawn from easily recognizable and fairly recent events in the dreamer's life. But there are also dreams that are much richer and complex in content, in which the images cannot so easily be related to normal waking life.

Despite the enormous amount of new material on dream content now available, no clear formula on interpretation of the content of dreams has yet emerged, though, a few general trends have been discerned. Deeply depressed people who are seriously contemplating suicide tend to have a particular type of dream, often one featuring a barren or desolate landscape. Thus the dreamer appears to be expressing, not the suicidal thought itself, but the feeling of isolation upon which the suicidal impulse is based. But this sort of interpretation is very general indeed.

It is entirely possible that dreaming is too much of an individualized matter to lend itself to broad interpretation. We are, in the view of psychiatrist Erich Fromm, the authors of our own dreams and we draw upon a vast store of material. Dreams are created out of our emotions, our cultural values and perceptions, but they also are influenced by our biology, our chemistry, and our inherited physical structure. They may also, it seems, be influenced by the hardness of our mattress or the pizza that we had for dinner that evening.

Sleep cuts us off from most outside stimuli, and may make us more acutely aware of what is going on inside us. This awareness can be expressed in our dreams. There is some evidence that hints of certain illness like heart attacks can sometimes be found in the dreams of the potential victim. This may be because the sleeper is able to recognize unconsciously the mild physical signs of an impending illness that pass unnoticed during a busy waking life. It is equally possible that the waking person is at least marginally aware of these signs and their meaning, but suppresses or denies this knowledge when awake. The repressed realization may surface during dreaming when the mind is no longer subjected to strict conscious controls.

So dreams can potentially reveal something about our inner world, both mental and physical, but do they have anything to reveal about the outer world? Do dreams put us in touch with the minds of others, with distant places, or the future, or with God? This of course was the commonly held view up to the present century. Freud had even toyed with the idea of precognitive or telepathic dreams, but had rejected it. Most, though not all, psychiatrists followed Freud's lead and were uninterested in looking for evidence of ESP in dreams. Most of the early sleep and dream researchers held essentially the same opinion. They either didn't believe in ESP or felt that their research was not the proper place in which to look for the evidence.

Yet people had certainly not stopped having dreams that they considered telepathic, precognitive or extrasensory in some other way. One modern parapsychologist has observed that "Sixty-five percent of spontaneous ESP experiences [those not occurring in a laboratory or under monitored conditions] take place in dreams."

Since they began, the various psychical research organizations have collected an enormous number of accounts of individuals who claimed that they had extrasensory dreams of one sort or another.

Dr. Ian Stevenson of the University of Virginia has collected and published a number of accounts of individuals who believed that they had in one way or another foreseen the sinking of the *Titanic*. The *Titanic*, the largest and fastest passenger ship of its time, struck an iceberg and sank in the North Atlantic during her maiden voyage on April 14, 1912. More than 1,500 of the 2,207 passengers and crew died in the catastrophe. It was surely the most tragic and spectacular ship sinking of modern times.

Fifty years after the disaster Dr. Stevenson, rereading newspapers and journals of the time, discovered that a lot of people claimed that they had foreseen the disaster. The most numerous, as well as the most remarkable, of these premonitions (if that's what they were) came in dreams.

An Englishwoman, Mrs. Charles Hughes, who was a child at the time of the sinking, recalled that on the night of April 12, 1912, she was staying with her grandmother, when she experienced "the most vivid dream I ever had." She saw herself on a road and observed "a very large ship a short distance away . . ." with "figures walking about on it, and I just stood wondering what it was doing there and suddenly it lowered one end and I heard a terrific scream."

She woke up and related the dream to her grandmother, who was both bothered and a bit frightened by it. Mrs. Hughes then recalls, "After a while I must have gone to sleep again and saw the very same scene, and when the people screamed I must have done. Gran was real livid with me this time and said I wasn't stopping with her again at night."

As it turned out, one of Mrs. Hughes' uncles had been the *Titanic's* fourth engineer and died in the disaster, though at the time apparently no one in the family knew that the uncle was aboard the ship, and found out only after news of the sinking had been published.

Even more striking was the case of J. Cannon Middleton,

a British businessman who booked passage on the *Titanic* on March 23. Ten days before sailing he had a dream of the ship "floating on the sea, keel upwards and her passengers and crew swimming around her." The next night he had the same dream, and the dreams so depressed and frightened him that he canceled his reservation after a cable from the United States advised him that for business reasons he should postpone his departure anyway for a few days. After he canceled the reservation, he told his friends and family about his dreams, and when the disaster took place, he sent an account of the entire incident to the British Society for Psychical Research.

Similar prophetic dreams have been reported regarding other dramatic and startling events. Many people have reported having premonitions of the assassination of President John F. Kennedy in dreams.

Striking and dramatic as accounts of such prophetic dreams are, as hard evidence they suffer from grievous shortcomings. The most damaging thing about such accounts is that they are usually written down only after the prophesied event has actually occurred. Thus the person who consciously or unconsciously wishes to alter the content of the dream to make it sound more prophetic is free to do so. Could so many people of apparently sound mind and good character be engaged in deliberate lying? Some of them certainly could, and did, but deliberate falsification is not necessarily an explanation. There appears to be an almost universal human tendency to alter our recollection of personal events to make them appear more significant and interesting than they really were.

We all possess highly selective memories. Psychologists have found that in a group that has listened to the same speech or witnessed the same event, individuals usually

EXTRASENSORY DREAMING

remember different details or stress certain details. Generally the details that are remembered best are those which support the opinions the individual already holds.

This problem is particularly acute in the case of dreams, for as we have already pointed out, our morning-after memory of dreams is notoriously poor. In my own lifetime I have remembered about a half dozen dreams which I considered particularly vivid and interesting (though not prophetic). I have repeated accounts of these dreams many times, and it has been pointed out to me that the dreams seem to get better and more dramatic with each retelling. That is probably true, though I am certain that I never deliberately set out to falsify the story; it just seemed to come out that way.

We also confront the problem of coincidence and interpretation. Is it really so improbable that a man about to embark on a long sea voyage should dream of a sinking ship? The fact that the ship actually did sink may just be coincidence. It is impossible to calculate what the odds against this sort of "prophetic" dream coming true by pure chance are. But if one balances the reported cases of dreams that come true against those in which the "prophetic" dreams failed to come true, it would seem most unwise to rule out the explanation of chance.

Chance is also a reasonable explanation for the most famous of all prophetic dreams in American history—the dream of assassination that President Abraham Lincoln was supposed to have had a few days before he was shot. Prior to his assassination there had been dozens of threats upon the President's life. Lincoln, a melancholy and deeply fatalistic man, must surely have worried about such threats, even dreamed of them. It is, in fact, highly unlikely that he would not have.

And then there is the problem of interpretation. So often

our dreams are murky and puzzling and so obscure that we can make of them what we will. A few years ago a psychical researcher showed me a case from his records of a dream that he considered highly prophetic. The subject had dreamed of an airplane going down on an island amid palm trees and "Egyptian-type statues." A week later there was a disastrous plane crash on the island of Cyprus. This researcher pointed to the dream of the crash, the island and the warm setting as indications of prophecy. As for the "Egyptian-type statues," he concluded that the dreamer had misinterpreted his own dream and would have been more accurate if he had reported "ancient statues." Cyprus is a land with a long history, and while not noted for its ancient statuary, certainly has some. But it seemed to me that this researcher was stretching a point and interpreting the record to fit the event after it occurred. Prophecy, it seems, was in the eyes of the beholder. As far as proof of precognition, or any other form of extrasensory perception in dreams, that sort of looseness is thoroughly unsatisfactory.

One could go through all the records of incidents of precognition, telepathy or clairvoyance in dreams, and pick them apart, as I have just done, and then dismiss the entire subject as unworthy of further attention. This is perhaps what the confirmed skeptic should do. And yet, is it really quite fair or wise to simply brush aside all of those reports because they are puzzling or incomplete? No, it isn't, because spontaneous events, like purported extrasensory dreams, are by their very nature incompletely and inaccurately reported. This does not necessarily mean that they are utterly without value. All it means is that this type of spontaneous experience is not the kind that can ever be used as conclusive proof.

While there had been attempts to make laboratory studies of other types of extrasensory events, it appeared as though dreams, by their very nature, would have to remain in the realm of spontaneous events. That at least, is how it appeared until the study of sleep and dreams entered the laboratory in the late 1950s.

As we said, the pioneer sleep and dream researchers were not specifically interested in dream content, and particularly not in testing possible extrasensory effects in dreams. It wasn't until 1963 that a division of parapsychology was established at Maimonides and work on the extrasensory elements in dreams began in earnest.

Even its most ardent supporters admit that ESP lacks a basic theory to explain how it works. There is even considerable disagreement over what conditions are supposed to make the ESP effect stronger. But if there is any general agreement in the field, it is that people are more sensitive to extrasensory perceptions—be they telepathic, clairvoyant or precognitive—at a time when the ordinary senses are quiet.

In this theory or model of how extrasensory perception works, the mind is seen as a sort of radio receiver. Under usual conditions it is assailed constantly by "sensory noise," sights, sounds, smells, even thoughts. Any psi or psychic perceptions would be blocked by all of this interference. Some theorists contend that the development of human language, followed by later developments in communication, writing, telephones, television, et cetera, reduced the human need for psi abilities, and they have begun to atrophy from disuse in modern man. But in moments of meditation, reverie or sleep these ancient psi impressions are more likely to be recognized. The fact that a high percentage of spontaneous ESP cases are reported at just such times lends considerable weight to the theory.

The Maimonides researchers set out first to test the most well-known and respectable of the presumed ESP abilities, telepathy, the communication of a message or image from one mind to another. The percipient or receiver in these experiments is chosen from among individuals who members of the lab staff feel have demonstrated extrasensory abilities. About half the volunteers pass preliminary telepathy tests, and occasionally a "sensitive" of some reputation is recruited for tests. Today the percipients are paid a modest $50 for five nights of having their dreams monitored.

The percipient is wired up so that his brain waves and eye movements can be monitored, thus letting the researchers know when he is dreaming, and put to bed in a soundproofed room. In a room in a different part of the hospital sits the agent or sender, another volunteer or member of the staff. The agent is given a picture, usually a reproduction of a painting, and during the night attempts to transmit this picture by thought to the sleeping percipient. Naturally the percipient is not told what picture is being used as the target. The Maimonides researchers chose to work with paintings rather than the simple symbols on an ESP card, or a series of numbers, because they felt that such stark images lacked a richness and emotional content that is conducive to the psi experience. The problem, as Maimonides workers will acknowledge, is that the results of the experiment are more ambiguous than they would be with a simple symbol or number.

During the night the sleeper is awakened at the end of each dream and asked to recount it into a microphone linked to a bedside tape recorder. The following morning there is a dream review where the sleeper again retells what he can remember of the night's dreams. Sometimes the sleeper is shown six pictures, including the target picture, and asked if any seemed familiar to him from his dreams. The dream reports are also submitted to an independent panel of judges, usually individuals who are not directly connected with the dream laboratory, to guard against possible bias of interpretation.

The judges have a scale upon which they rate the correspondence between a night's dream and the target picture. Sometimes the judges will also be given a half dozen pictures without being told which is the target. Oddly, judges appear to be better at finding a correspondence between the pictures and the dreams than are the dreamers themselves. In a 1968 study, subjects linked their dreams and target pictures in only 64 percent of the cases, a figure that dream lab researchers felt was not quite statistically significant. Judges, on the other hand, linked written reports of the same dreams with targets in 91 percent of the cases—definitely a statistically significant figure. Researchers felt that one of the reasons that the judges did so well was that they had a chance to review the dream reports at leisure, whereas the dreamers did not have an opportunity to look over their own reports, and had to depend solely on memory.

There is, however, another possible explanation as to why the judges are so much better at picking target pictures than are the dreamers themselves. During the limited period in which the actual experiment is being carried out, it would be relatively easy to maintain tight controls, that is, to keep the subject from finding out the target picture. After the dream review, however, the experimenters would almost inevitably relax a bit. Time would pass during which transcripts of the dream reports are prepared and the pictures are collected and given to the judges. The possibility of the judges' finding out which of the pictures they were shown was really the target would be far higher than they would be for the subject. Anyone who has ever worked in a small office knows how hard it is to keep a secret—any secret. I have no proof that the results are due to careless office procedure rather than ESP; indeed, such a suggestion may be quite wrong. But it must be considered.

The transcript of dreams tends to be lengthy and rambling. A dream recall record for a single night may run anywhere from twenty-five to seventy typewritten pages. Often nothing in the record can be related to the target picture, even by the most generous interpretation. But in others the correspondence has been striking.

In one celebrated case in the early 1960s the target painting was called "Animals," by the Japanese artist Tamayo. This painting showed a pair of hungry-looking dogs standing over some bones. In the background was a large black rock. The subject described dreaming: "I was eating something like rib steak. And this friend of mine was there. People were talking about how she wasn't very good to invite to dinner because she was very conscious of other people getting more to eat than she got, especially meat." The phrase "black rock" was used several times, and the subject spoke of "that mermaid from the Black Rock bar . . ."

For another dreamer the target painting was George Bellows' interpretation of the Dempsey and Firpo boxing match. The dreamer reported repeated images of boxing "Something about posts," he recalled. "There's a feeling of moving. Ah, something about Madison Square Garden and a boxing match." Later the same night he dreamed of "a square shape . . . two or three figures . . . and a presence of other people."

Van Gogh's painting, "Boats on the Beach," produced almost a direct hit. The subject reported dreaming of "being on a boardwalk or a beach . . . the seacoast. The place is slightly elevated . . . it makes me think of Van Gogh."

Occasionally an apparently spontaneous psychic event

takes place right in the middle of an experiment. On Friday, July 20, 1973, the subject being tested was Felicia Parise, a research associate in hematology at Maimonides, and one of the "stars" of the dream lab. She dreamed that she saw a co-worker looking at a copy of the New York *Daily News* with a picture of a collapsed building on the front page.

"Mark this one down, Steve," she said to Steve Goldfinger, who was monitoring her dreams; "it's precognitive."

Two weeks later, on Friday, August 3, the old Broadway Central Hotel collapsed, and the *News* ran a huge picture of the wreckage on its front page.

Miss Parise's dream, like the precognitive dreams reported about the sinking of the *Titanic* and the assassination of President Kennedy, concerned an awesome and deeply emotional event—far more emotional than the standard ESP symbols or than the paintings used in the Maimonides tests. In order to raise the emotional content of their targets, the dream lab researchers have tried an enormous number of techniques ranging from the ingenious to the bizarre.

One method of reinforcing or enriching the target picture was to present the agent with scenes, music or objects that were related to it. With a picture called "Downpour at Shono," which shows a Japanese man with an umbrella trying to escape a driving rain, the agent was given a toy Japanese umbrella. The dreamer reported images of fountains and rain.

In another picture, "The Descent from the Cross," the agent was given a crucifix, a picture of Jesus and, almost sacrilegiously, several thumbtacks. This time the dreamer described an emaciated figure and a god who spoke through sacrificial victims.

One of the hallmarks of the Maimonides dream lab staff is their willingness to try almost anything. One of their more unusual and spectacular attempts came early in 1971. A popular rock group called The Grateful Dead was giving a concert in Port Chester, New York, some 45 miles away from the dream laboratory. The group had earlier visited Dr. Krippner at the laboratory and expressed interest in his work. They agreed to try a long-distance ESP experiment with the concert audience acting as the telepathic agents. If a single agent could project an image successfully, several hundred might be even better at projecting the image.

The percipient was to be Malcolm Bessent, a British psychic who had already participated very successfully in several of the dream lab's other tests. The audience was shown a different slide each night. The slide was projected for about fifteen minutes, while The Grateful Dead continued to play. The audience was told that they were taking part in an ESP experiment and that they were supposed to try to "send" the picture to Malcolm Bessent.

In their book *Dream Telepathy* Ullman and Krippner report, "Observers at the concerts noted that the majority of the audience were already in altered states of consciousness by target time. These altered states were brought about by the music, or by the earlier ingestion of psychedelic drugs, or by contact with the other members of the audience."

In addition to Bessent there was a "control" subject, about whom the audience knew nothing. She was Felicia Parise, a psychic star but not as much of a star as Bessent. She was not in the laboratory, but spent the night at her apartment and was telephoned every 90 minutes for dream reports. Dreams occur at roughly 90-minute intervals during a normal night's sleep.

The most interesting direct correspondence between dream and target picture occurred on February 19, 1971. The slide shown to the audience was "The Seven Spinal

Chakras," a painting showing a man meditating in the lotus position. The seven chakras (supposedly the energy centers of the body centering around the spinal column) are vividly colored. There is a brilliant yellow circle radiating from the head of the meditating figure in a pattern of mosaic facets.

Excerpts from Malcolm Bessent's dream of that evening read:

"I was very interested in . . . using natural energy . . . I was talking to this guy who said he'd invented a way of using solar energy and he showed me this box . . . to catch the light from the sun which was all we needed to generate and store the energy . . . I was discussing with this other guy a number of other areas of communication and we were exchanging ideas on the whole thing . . . He was suspended in midair or something . . . I was thinking about rocket ships . . . I'm remembering a dream I had . . . about an energy box and . . . a spinal column."

In her apartment that same night Felicia Parise was dreaming, "I had a big, fat, yellowish, green parakeet with a head like an owl. Something happened to the cage and it broke . . . I also had another dream with a yellow canary . . . The cage was hanging very high outside of the garage door . . . I said, 'I wonder how the parakeet lives? I never feed it. God must raise his temperature so he doesn't freeze.' "

Two nights later, though, on February 21, a most remarkable thing happened. Miss Parise had a dream which appeared to correspond much more closely to the target of "The Seven Spinal Chakras" shown on February 19. "It was something bright, like a crystal with many facets of colors . . . There is some sort of light or sun or bright light. It's maybe a man, short like a Buddha . . . like something Aztec, a Mexican totem pole."

When the transcripts of the dream reports, along with the target pictures, were sent to two independent judges and rated on a 100-point scale, the judges gave a mean score of 83 for Bessent's dream on February 19. Miss Parise's dream of the same night, the one with the yellow parakeet, was given only a 28. But her dream of February 21 was rated at 96, a near-perfect score, on the correspondence scale to the picture of February 19.

By the scoring system set up for the tests, Bessent had four "hits" out of the six nights of testing with the concert audience, while Miss Parise had only one. But on some of the nights that she missed the target, her dreams were given high correspondence to targets shown on other nights. Her 96 rating on "The Seven Spinal Chakras" dream was the highest scored during the entire test series by either subject. Comment Ullman and Krippner, "These are all in the Great Correspondence to the Very Great Correspondence range, and they suggest that she may have been displacing her ESP in time—both backward (postcognitively) and forward (precognitively)."

One tentative conclusion that the Maimonides researchers drew from this series of experiments is that it didn't seem to make much difference if there were 2000 agents, as there were in the concert audience, or a single one, as in more conventional dream lab experiments. Nor did distance appear to make any difference. The results were just about the same.

Another novel attempt to raise the emotional "energy" of an experiment is to immerse the agent in an "audo-visual environment." This is a technique developed by Drs. R. E. L. Masters and Jean Houston, researchers much interested in altered states of consciousness. The audio-visual environment consists of a sequence of slides projected on an 8-foot screen that curves around the subject. The subject is also seated between stereo loudspeakers, or wears a headset, which blares out appropriate music and sounds. A computerized dual slide projector dissolves one slide into another every twenty seconds, giving the impression of a "moving picture." The over-all effect is so powerful that the subject can reach a "sensory overload," and enter what Masters and Houston call an altered state of consciousness, in which the subject experiences profound emotional feelings, and even mystical and religious experiences.

In a group of experiments which ran from April to December, 1969, a series of telepathic agents sat in the Masters and Houston laboratory at the Foundation for Mind Research in New York City, engulfed in their audio-visual environments. Fourteen miles away, in Brooklyn, two subjects were asleep in the dream laboratory, and trying to telepathically pick up the content of the audo-visual environment.

All of the audio-visual environments have a theme. Typical was "Space Exploration." The slide program included views of the astronauts, slides of the Apollo 11 flight, the moon landing and the return trip. One dreamer that night reported "silver and bright colors"; "travel"; "futuristic designs for suits"; "getting ready for a long trip"; and "traveling to distant points." Three judges who were later given the dream transcripts and six possible topics with which to relate them, all picked the subject "Space Exploration" as number one.

In another test the target subject was "Ancient Egypt," with slides of the pyramids, sphinxes, statues, ruins, temples, paintings, and articles from the tomb of Tutankhamen. The dreamer reported "a semi-tropical setting" and "statuary and paintings. It was in an institute where a lot of people were studying . . . something to do with death . . . Beautiful art, gardens, sculpture, and fountains . . ." The judges rated "Ancient Egypt" number two out of six possible choices.

When the dreamer was Douglas Johnson, a well-known British medium, the randomly chosen program was "Oriental Religion." The slides showed Buddhas from a number of different countries, as well as various Indian and Tibetan deities. The accompanying sound was the chanting of Zen Buddhist monks and Sufi religious rituals. Johnson dreamed: "I saw rather a beautiful face—squarish with slanty eyes. Eastern, I would think. Clean-shaven . . . I don't know what nationality, but it was a very beautiful face."

The second dreaming subject that night was a young lady named Susan, who had no prior ESP experiences. She dreamed: "Something about people who didn't believe in God any more and the sun came down to earth to find out why . . . And Richie came later dressed in like these robes —white robes with blue stitching on them . . ." and adding later, "It could have been like some sort of religious theme."

The judges gave number one correspondence to the subject of "Oriental Religion" for both the dreams of Susan and Douglas Johnson. It may seem a bit surprising that someone who had shown no psychic abilities at all should do as well, and perhaps even a bit better than a professional psychic. The reason, the Maimonides researchers feel, was the Richie mentioned in the dream. He was Richard Davidson, a staff research associate and the agent for that night's session. He also happened to be Susan's boyfriend. Ask Ullman and Krippner, "Did the stronger emotional rapport between Richard and Susan enable Susan to dream as telepathically as a professional psychic?"

One of the most familiar and frequently reported psi experiences is the prophetic dream—dreaming about something that has not yet happened. With the wealth of anecdo-

EXTRASENSORY DREAMING 109

tal material available on this subject, it is a concept that certainly deserved testing, but devising an adequate test for prophetic dreaming was a project which taxed the ingenuity of the dream lab staff.

What they finally came up with was an experiment that worked this way. The subject would go to sleep in the standard laboratory manner. After his night's dreams were recorded, a member of the staff would choose a number out of a table of random numbers. The number was used to pick a word out of a book called *Content Analysis of Dreams,* and the word was then matched up with an art-print target, and the art target used to design a whole multi-sensory environment to which the dreamer would be subjected late in the morning after he had done his dreaming.

Here is how the system worked in practice. The dreaming subject was Malcolm Bessent, the psychic who claimed credit for predicting a number of important and unexpected news events, and who was extensively tested at Maimonides.

During his second dream one night Bessent recalled, "There was a large concrete building. A lot of concrete . . . and there was a patient from upstairs, I'm not sure it was a 'he.' It might have been a woman . . . She had a white coat on like a doctor's coat and people were arguing with her on the street."

From the third dream: "Kind of a feeling. Not a feeling exactly, but a rumor . . . of hostility toward me by people in a group I was in daily contact with . . . My impression was that they were doctors and medical people . . ."

In his fourth dream he said, "The cups were all white . . ."

In the morning Dr. Krippner was given a random number. He used this to choose a key word from the dream book. The word was "corridor." Using this word, he selected the Van Gogh picture "Hospital Corridor at St. Remy." This picture shows a figure in the corridor of a mental institution. The corridor is constructed of concrete.

For the multi-sensory environment, Krippner devised a little drama in which Malcolm Bessent was the unwitting star. The psychic was taken by two burly hospital attendants down a darkened corridor to Krippner's office. In the office a slide projector flashed drawings made by mental patients on the wall, while a tape recorder played the weird theme music from the movie "Spellbound." Behind the desk sat Krippner, who proceeded to address Bessent (whom he knew quite well) as Mr. Van Gogh. Every once in a while Krippner would laugh hysterically. Bessent was given a pill to swallow, and his face was daubed with a cotton swab.

The corridor dreams were considered to be a "direct hit" and one of the best correspondences ever found in the years of Maimonides experiments.

But probably the most striking example of apparently precognitive dreaming by Malcolm Bessent took place on September 13, 1970. In this experiment Bessent was instructed to try to dream about a series of slides to be chosen at random later, and shown to him the following night. On September 14, Bessent was shown a series of slides of birds. The night before he had dreamed of a parapsychologist who had previously worked with birds.

"His experiments with birds. The general reaction to him would be of his interest, I felt . . . The target is of emotional interest to [him]."

In reviewing his dreams the following morning, but before he was shown the slides, Bessent talked extensively of birds: "I remember seeing various different kinds of doves. Ringtailed doves, ordinary doves, Canadian geese. There were many, many different kinds of varieties."

Judges comparing the transcripts of Bessent's dream record with the subject gave it a correlation score of 98 out of a possible 100, nearly a perfect correlation and one of the highest scores ever achieved in any of the Maimonides dream studies. And in this series remember that Malcolm Bessent was supposed to be dreaming about something that had not yet happened.

This is the sort of experience that parapsychologists find both exciting and disturbing. It is possible to work out a generally acceptable theory for telepathy, that is, mind-to-mind communication. Precognition, however, presents a far more complex theoretical problem, and one that has really never been adequately tackled. And yet time after time, we find that the evidence for precognition is every bit as good as it is for telepathy, and in some cases, like the birds series just cited, it is better.

What is one to make of all this? Drs. Ullman and Krippner and most of those associated with the dream lab were confirmed believers in ESP even before they had started their dream laboratory work. The aim of the laboratory was not to prove the existence of psi abilities, but rather to explore them and find out how they can best be tested. But others have looked upon the mass of work stretching over a series of many years, and have concluded that as a whole the Maimonides experiments do provide the long-sought-after conclusive proof of ESP.

But the traditional critics of ESP research have not been won over or silenced by the mass of research conducted in the Brooklyn hospital. The first problem that they raise is the one of the repeatable experiment. In one sense, the very success and ingenuity of the Maimonides staff may be a severe drawback. Maimonides has at its command more equipment, time and far more money than many other laboratories which might be interested in ESP research. For that reason alone, the research is hard to duplicate.

Then there is the matter of atmosphere. ESP researchers have long contended that enthusiastic belief in ESP helps to promote high scores on ESP tests. This means not only that the agent and subject in an experiment should believe in ESP, but that the researchers and staff workers also have a positive attitude. If researchers act suspicious, as though they expected someone to cheat, then, say ESP enthusiasts, the delicate contact appears to break down, and one gets poor test results.

Dr. David Foulkes, who tried two not very successful replication studies of dream telepathy at the University of Wyoming, commented, "In retrospect, we may have erred too much on the side of 'scientism' to the exclusion of creating conditions in which telepathy might reasonably (if it exists at all) be expected to flourish. It proved hard to escape the role of protector of scientific purity, guardian of scientific morals. Were we sympathetic and encouraging observers, or scientific detectives out to prevent a crime from being committed before our very eyes? Sometimes it was difficult to be certain."

So there are both physical and what might be called psychological difficulties in repeating the Maimonides experiments. Replication is necessary in dream telepathy studies, just as it is in all other laboratory experiments. For one thing we must be sure that the encouraging Maimonides atmosphere does not also include sloppy procedure and allow what parapsychologists may euphemistically call "sensory leakage." There are many ways, quite innocent ones, by which a subject could get a hint as to what the target is, or an experimenter might choose a target which is known to be of interest to the subject and that he might very likely be dreaming about anyway.

The experimenter, that is, the individual who is actually monitoring the recording of the dreams, could also influence the content of the dream recall. Transcripts of full dream records show that the experimenter often prompts dream recall by asking the subject to repeat something or explain something. Such prompting almost certainly influences what the dreamer says to some extent. If the experimenter knew the subject of the target, then it would be nearly inevitable that he would ask the subject to repeat things that sounded like they might relate to that target. This would cause the subject to stress those dream elements which might be related to the target, and play down those which appeared irrelevant. Indeed, under such prompting a subject eager to get a "hit" might be tempted to say things that he has never actually dreamed about. I have already mentioned the possibility of judges finding out the target picture in an experiment.

I am not trying to say that such things do happen—merely that they could. This is one way in which the results of the studies could be incorrect without any actual cheating being involved. And, of course, one cannot rule out the possibility of actual cheating in some cases. Cheating in all branches of scientific research is a good deal more common than the layman suspects. That is a major reason why repeatable experiments are so important. Cheating has been particularly rampant in the field of psychical research, and it will be necessary for experiments to be successfully repeated by skeptics as well as believers.

There is another and even more basic problem, however. This concerns the interpretation of the significance of the dream material. The experiments as they have been related here often sound impressive. But an average dream report runs anywhere from twenty-five to seventy typewritten pages. From this mass of material only a few words or a few sentences at most may be considered significant in relating the dream to the target picture. In some cases like Bessent's dream of birds, and the bird slide show, the relationship is obvious; in others it is more difficult to discern any clear relationship. Most of the recorded dreams and dream reviews are utterly irrelevant to the target. In other cases the dream may really be relevant to something other than the target. Malcolm Bessent's dream of the hospital surroundings may have had less to do with the Van Gogh hospital picture that was his target than with the fact that he was being tested in a hospital at that time. Rather than having a precognitive dream about what was going to happen the next day, he may have had a perfectly ordinary dream about his surroundings.

There is also a disturbing tendency to change experimental design to fit the results. Recall The Grateful Dead study—when Miss Parise's dream of February 21 seemed to relate very closely to the slide shown on February 19. This was touted as being highly significant (and the correspondence does seem quite remarkable), but the experiment was not originally designed to test retrocognition. Changing it makes an impressive story but plays hell with over-all statistical analysis. It would also have been quite easy for Miss Parise to learn what slide had been shown two days earlier.

The whole setup is so complicated, delicate and subjective that a small error at any one of a thousand points could render a painstakingly prepared test meaningless.

The Maimonides research has not come up with a way of producing a subject who will dream absolutely on target night after night, any more than the old card calling tests ever located the individual who could go through the entire deck correctly time after time.

Dr. Donald J. West, a British psychiatrist and long-time critical investigator of parapsychology, has commented: "The one thought that occurs to me is that the dream techniques for eliciting ESP produce results which, on statistical standards, are about the same level as the traditional card calling tests. This means that in order to obtain answers to research questions you need to do a great many experiments and involve yourself in an enormous amount of labour. This is disappointing because one had hoped that the new technique would have released such a flood of ESP that tedious repetitions and statistical evaluations would no longer be required."

The material generated by the Maimonides experiments reminds me somewhat of the cross-correspondences. During the early years of the twentieth century, spirit mediums throughout the world began to report receiving messages from some of the founders of the Society for Psychical Research who had recently died. This was not in itself unusual or necessarily significant. What did seem significant, however, was that there appeared to be a correspondence between parts of a message received by one medium and something received by a second or a third. Often the mediums were in different parts of the world, and collusion between them would have been well-nigh impossible. These cross-correspondences went on for several years, and constituted what many believed (and some still do believe) was the best body of evidence for spirit return.

But there are some problems. The cross-correspondences are made up of thousands upon thousands of written pages of mediumistic communication (much of it, incidentally, has the same vague quality as transcribed dream reports). Correspondences can be found if one searches diligently enough for them, but usually they are so obscure, vague and in need of generous interpretation one wonders if there is really any correspondence at all. From this vast mass of material to draw from, it is not at all surprising that some correspondences could be found. But since the material was taken from many different individuals in different parts of the world, and since much of it appeared to relate to interests of the departed founders of the SPR, supporters believed that there was some kind of vast international word game being played by the spirits. Critics argued that the correspondences were coincidences, and the significance merely wishful thinking. There is no adequate way of resolving that question.

That is roughly where we are at with the Maimonides dream experiments. The fact that these experiments are conducted in a laboratory, rather than a darkened séance room, does not alter the vague and unsatisfactory quality of the evidence.

In the years since the Maimonides dream experiments were begun, they have generated a vast amount of data, a lot of it interesting, suggestive, and some fascinating and even eerie. They are deservedly the best-known ESP experiments going today. Perhaps someday we will look back upon them as providing a major breakthrough in the study of the basic nature of man. But for the present at least, they do not provide the long-sought conclusive experiment that ESP does indeed exist.

6
EXOTIC PSYCHIC PHENOMENA

DREAM research is the best-known psychic investigation now going, but it is certainly not the only one. Parapsychology or psychical research has gone way beyond the old card guessing days. Indeed it has gone well beyond the investigation of what used to be known as the big three plus one —telepathy, clairvoyance and precognition, plus psychokinesis, or mind over matter, which might or might not be related to the other three.

Today psychical research may include anything from "photographing" the human hand with high-voltage, high-frequency electricity to giving a lie detector test to a house plant.

What do these strange experiments have to do with what is commonly called extrasensory perception, or with the broader subject that Edgar Mitchell has called noetics, the study of human consciousness? Why should such exotica be of interest to parapsychologists?

There are two basic reasons. The first is that such phenomena lie beyond the borders of orthodox science; they tend to be ignored by what some consider to be the scientific

Establishment. Any odd phenomenon that has become a scientific stepchild is almost sure to rouse the sympathy of parapsychologists, who feel that they too have spent many years in the same scientific Siberia.

More significantly, though, each of these phenomena seems to hint that there is "something beyond" the material world as currently envisioned by science. It is important to keep in mind that the major thrust of parapsychology is not so much to discover a "sixth sense" or a "seventh" or "eighth sense," it is to prove that there are realities beyond the senses and that many of the philosophical assumptions of modern science are wrong. In truth, the philosophical assumptions of modern science are not nearly as rigid or universal as most of those interested in psychic subjects assume them to be. A lot of what psychical researchers inveigh against is nineteenth-century philosophy, which no longer carries weight in the light of twentieth-century knowledge.

This, however, is not meant to imply that orthodox science has "come around" to a point of view more sympathetic to the psychic.

There remains a distinct difference in approach between most orthodox scientists and scientists and others interested in psychic subjects. The more orthodox scientist does not often ask questions like "What is the nature of the universe?" or "What is the nature of man?" It is not because he lacks interest in such basic questions, but rather because he sees no way of finding an answer to them at our present state of knowledge. Scientist and novelist C. P. Snow has said, "Scientists regard it as a major intellectual virtue to know what not to think about." Scientists attack problems in which there seems a reasonable hope of finding an answer.

The person interested in the psychic finds such an attitude cowardly and almost criminal. To such an individual there

Captain Edgar D. Mitchell before the Apollo 14 flight.

Captain Mitchell discusses the results of his unofficial ESP test from space.

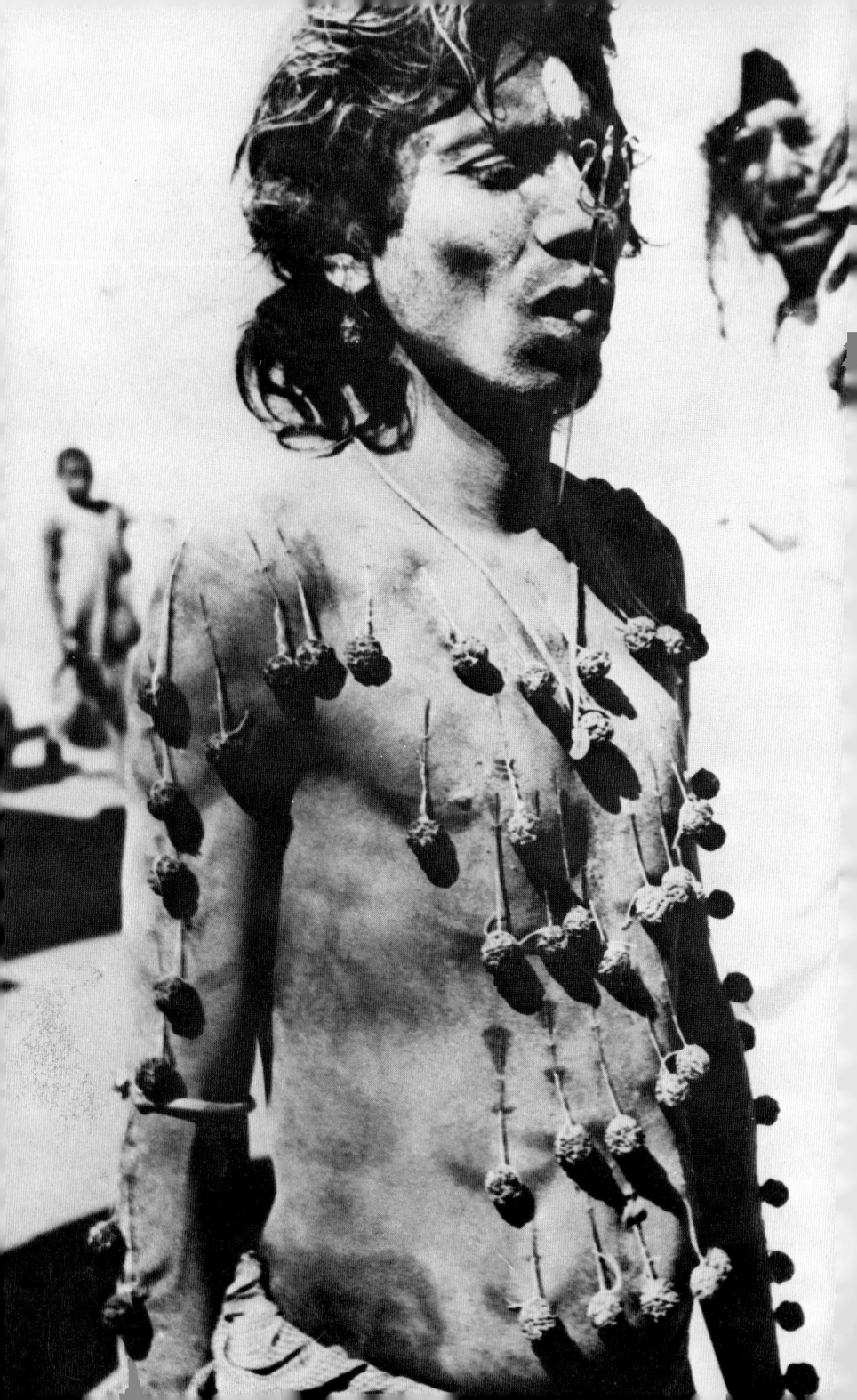

OPPOSITE: A Hindu holy man displays his indifference to pain during a religious festival. A sharp pin is struck through his tongue, and other pins with weights attached are embedded in his flesh.
UPI

RIGHT: This drawing of a European fakir with his trick swords and arrows demonstrates that a remarkable resistance to pain may be little more than a magical illusion.

Levitation is another ability commonly claimed by and for holy men of East and West.

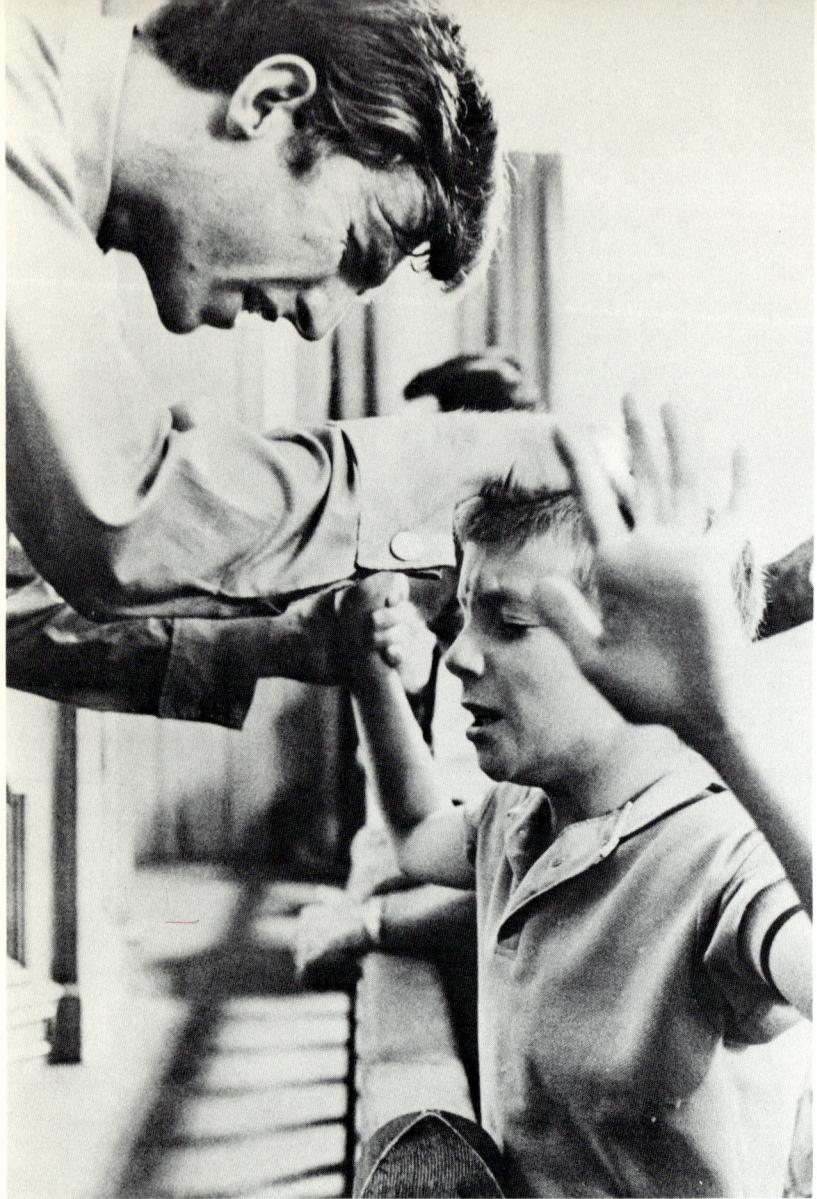
Religious News Service photo by Steve Dunwell

Healing by the laying on of hands is a regular feature in the services of many Pentecostal churches.

OPPOSITE TOP: An experiment in dream telepathy at the Maimonides dream laboratory. The subject has electrodes taped to her head in order to determine when she is dreaming.

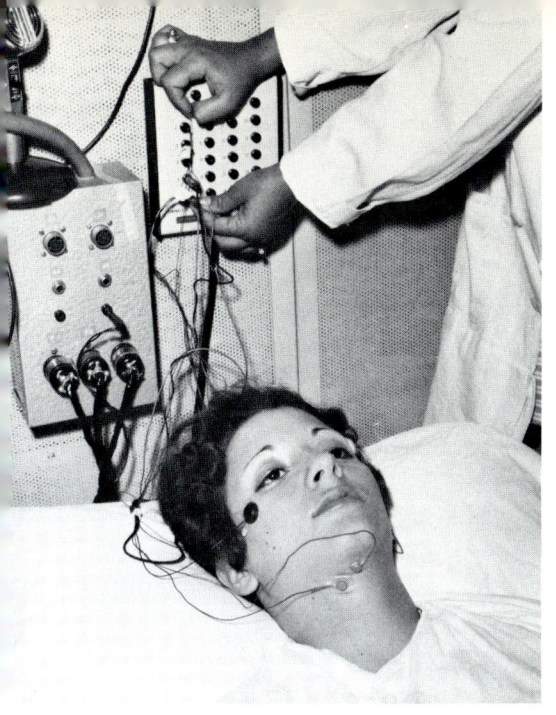

Both photos: Harold Friedman

BELOW: In another part of the laboratory the agent tries to transmit the target picture to the sleeping subject.

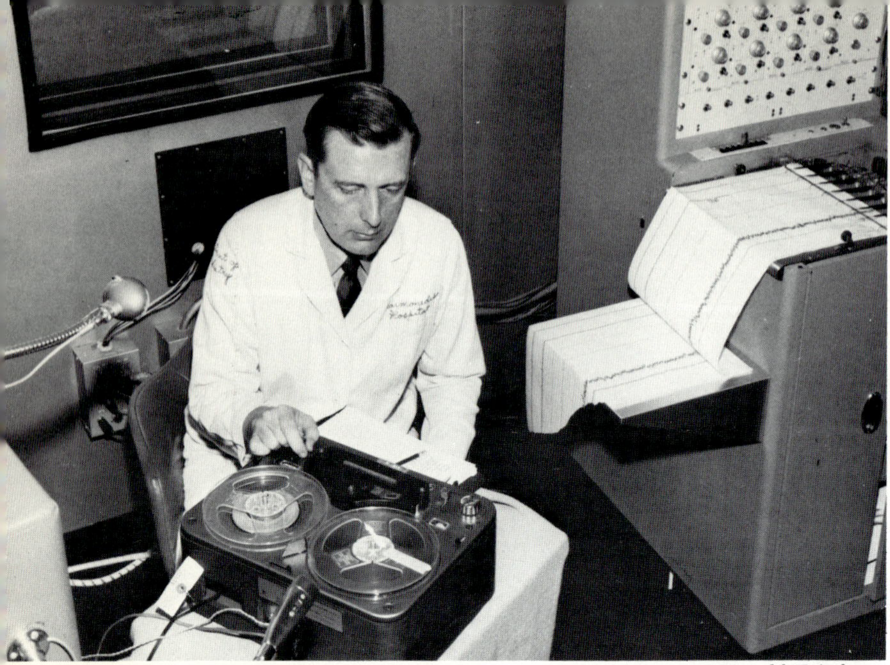

Harold Friedman

During the night the experimenter Dr. Stanley Krippner awakens the subject after a dream and asks her to record her recollections on tape.

The following morning a member of the laboratory staff asks the subject to pick the painting that corresponds most closely to her dreams.

Harold Friedman

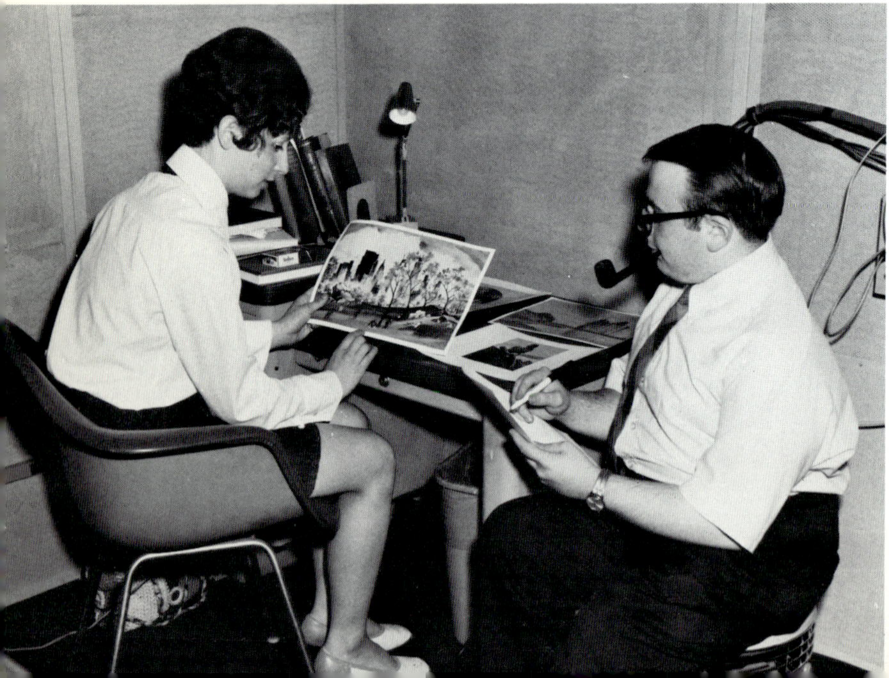

Experimental night 2, December 7, 1966
Target H, "Downpour at Shono," a painting by Hiroshige (detail)*

THIRD DREAM REPORT: "...something about an Oriental man who was ill...."

FIFTH DREAM REPORT: "The part I remember -- it sort of faded away but it had to do with fountains -- a big fountain. It would be like one you see in Italy. A fountain. Two images and a water spray that would shoot up. No color."

POST-SLEEP INTERVIEW: "There was a young man. He seemed to be an invalid or something, and he was on a bed. And I just don't remember any more.... I just had the two images this time, one with the fountain like the ones in Italy, the elaborate fountains, and a giant eye of a needle.... The fountain makes me think of pictures and scenes I've seen of Rome. In fact, a short time ago, I was looking at a book. The book is called 'Fountains in Italy,' I think. They have so many fountains.... I remember talking about fountains being renewing of life.... I was walking on the street. It seemed it was raining a little bit and we got to a particular point, and the street was blocked. So we had to walk out into the street and around.... Of course, it was raining, and it was night and it had a sort of heavy feeling...."

GUESS FOR THE NIGHT: "...in terms of just standing out, I would say the fountain and the needle.... Those particularly seem to sort of stand out as being unusual.... For some reason I'm going to say that it had something to do with...fountains or something.... Fountain. Maybe water...."

* The target picture portrays a Japanese man with an umbrella trying to escape a driving rain. The multisensory materials included a toy Japanese umbrella and the instructions to take a shower.

Science Digest

Significant sections from a dream report. Reports run from twenty-five to seventy pages.

Hospital Corridor at Saint Remy. (1889–90). Gouache and watercolor by Vincent Van Gogh. Collection, The Museum of Modern Art, N.Y. Abby Aldrich Rockefeller Bequest.

The target picture in a precognitive dream experiment. The subject dreamed of a hospital before this picture was chosen.

OPPOSITE: Early hypnotism or magnetism was a favorite subject for cartoonists. "Our faculties are in touch with each other," the magnetizer in this cartoon is saying to the donkey he is treating.

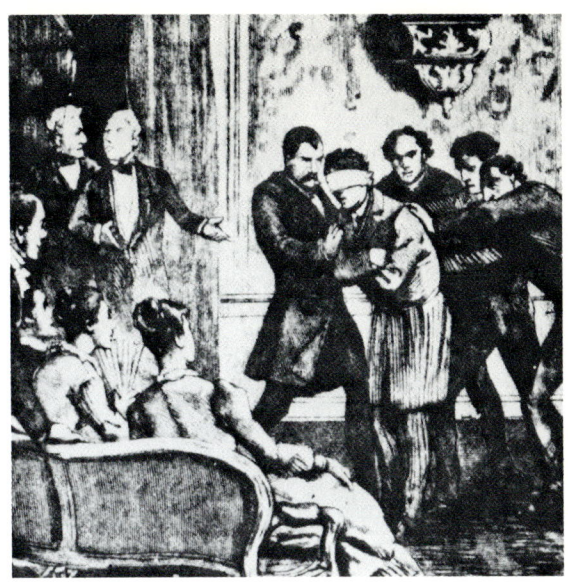

ABOVE: Parlor demonstrations of hypnotism were common during the nineteenth century. In France a man named Mirville tried to demonstrate that if a hypnotized subject received a "mental order" not to move, all efforts to make him do so would be unsuccessful.

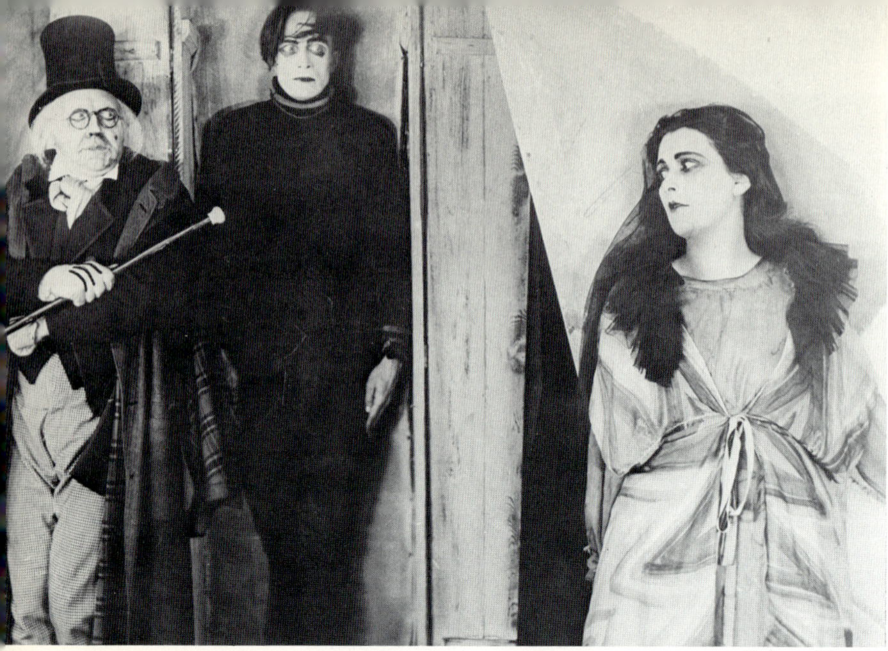

Culver Pictures

The sinister side of hypnotism has been a popular theme in fiction and movies. In the silent film classic *The Cabinet of Dr. Caligari* the evil hypnotist exercised absolute control over his zombie-like subject.

The astral body departing after death. From an early twentieth-century account of astral projection.

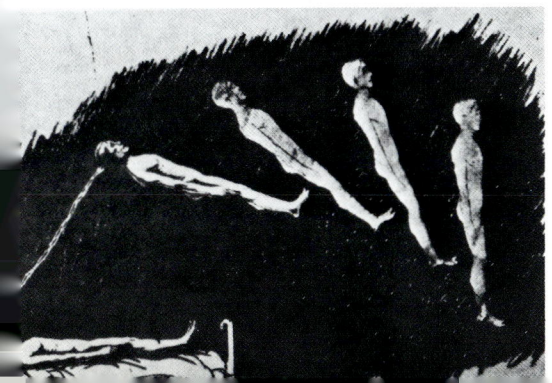

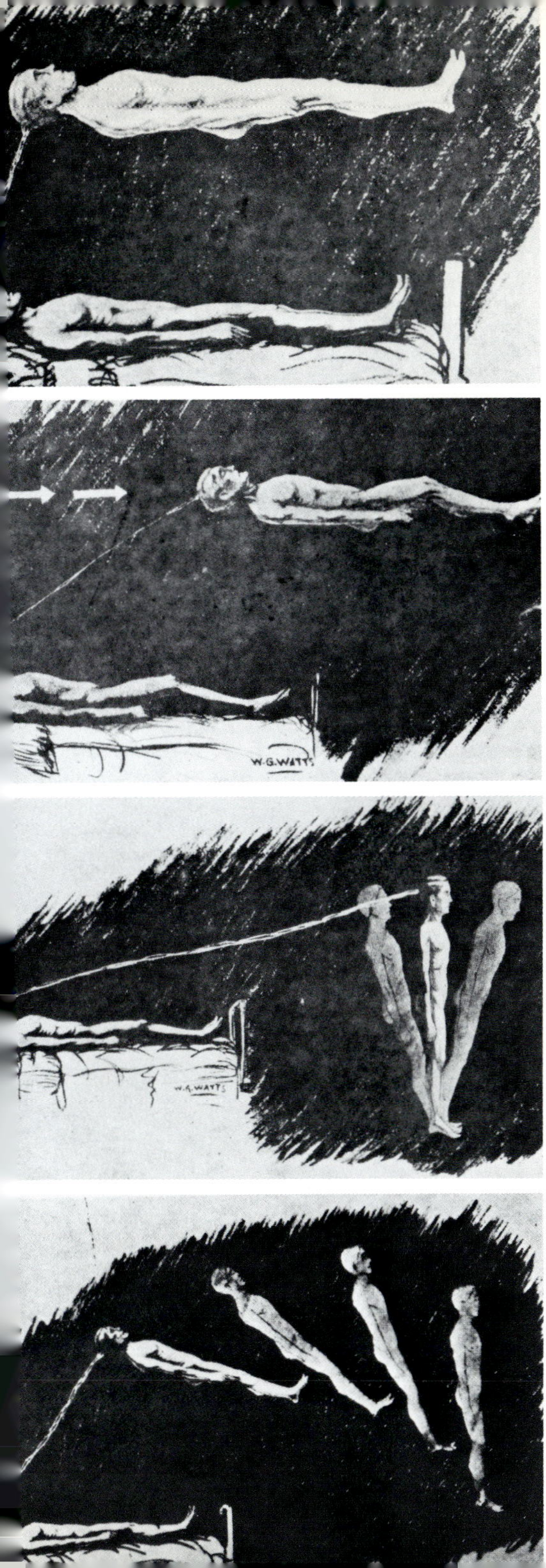

The early twentieth-century astral traveler Sylvan Muldoon believed that the astral body always remained connected to the physical body by an elastic "cord."

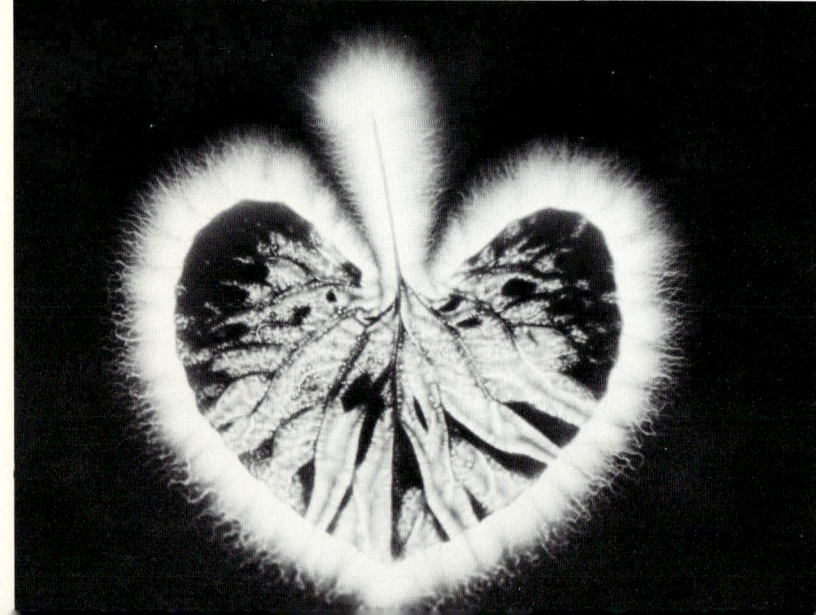

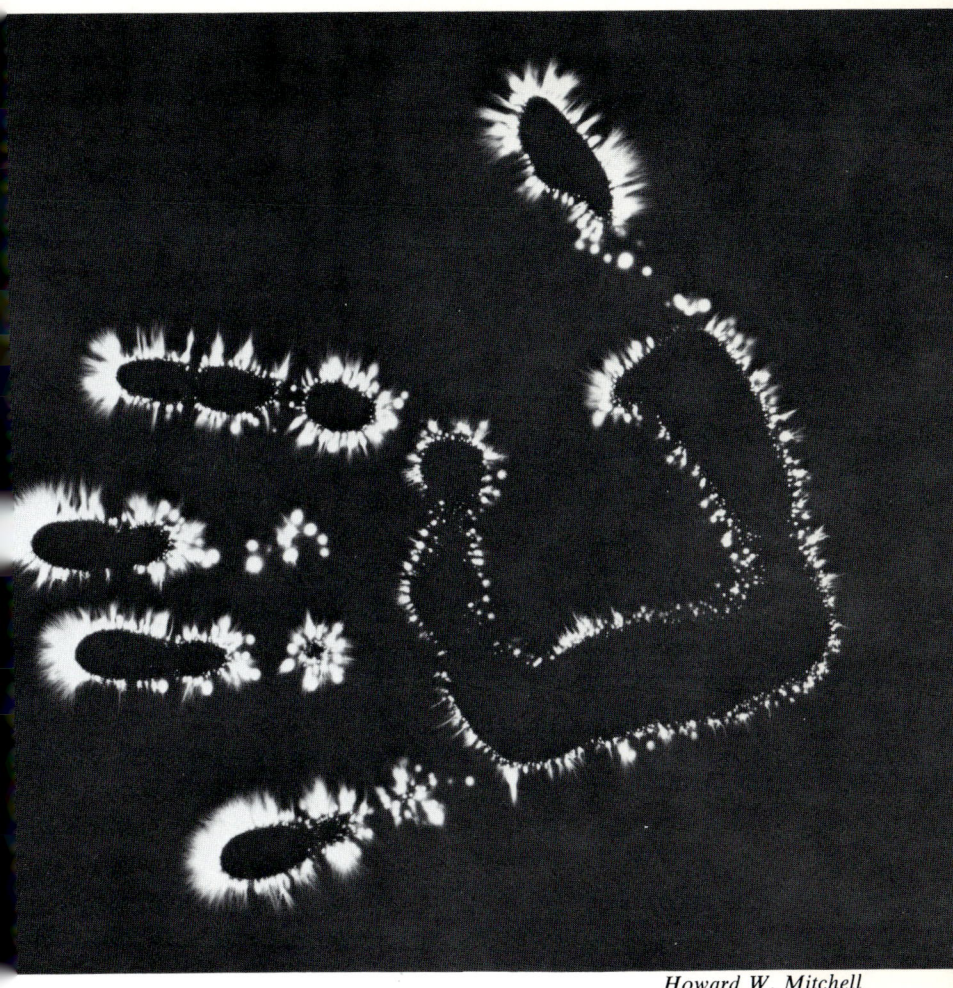

Howard W. Mitchell

Some believe Kirlian photos show the "aura" of living things. Others think the result is merely an oddity of the process itself. Howard W. Mitchell who took these photos says, "There are many, many variables which influence what one gets, and many of these variables are not related to what we think of as the mental state or psychic condition or whatever of the subject ... But: golly, Kirlian photos are fun to do!"

David Wilson

OPPOSITE: The Children of God during one of their dramatic demonstrations in Los Angeles. They have often been accused of brainwashing converts.

A young man stops playing the guitar and starts speaking in tongues during a charismatic renewal meeting at St. Columba Roman Catholic Church in Hopewell Junction, New York.
Religious News Service Photo by Chris Sheridan

Sir Alister Hardy

are no subjects that are "beyond useful investigation," even at our present state of knowledge. The big questions are the only questions really worth bothing about. No subject is too strange, too improbable to be worth an investigation. Who knows what might turn up? The gap between these two approaches is wide, deep and will probably never be reconciled. It accounts for much of the misunderstanding that arises between the center and the fringes of science. The orthodox scientist is appalled that the parapsychologist will plunge into yet one more investigation of a self-proclaimed psychic who says that he can bend keys just by thinking about it. A thousand times in the past similar claims have been proved fraudulent, much to the embarrassment of psychical researchers who had missed the trick. But the parapsychologist is always ready to take one more chance.

This characteristic willingness to try almost anything has recently led to some pretty exotic experiments, even in a field which is exotic by its very nature. With more instruments at their command the parapsychologists can cast their net more widely for phenomena that appear strange, unexplainable and perhaps psychic. We have already discussed how the use of physical monitoring equipment has revolutionized the study of ESP in dreams. In other areas a strange process called Kirlian photography is said to be producing concrete proof for a host of psychic phenomena that previously depended on vague and unsatisfactory accounts for support.

Kirlian photography is a technique first developed back in the 1930s by a Russian electronics specialist, Semyon Kirlian, and his wife. Kirlian would expose a subject to a small amount of high-voltage, high-frequency current and then "photograph" the subsequent electrical discharge by placing the subject up against a piece of film. Any subject can be used

—a coin, a piece of paper, a rubber band—but living subjects, a human hand, a leaf or bud have been the most popular. The resulting photograph shows the object surrounded by a weird-looking multi-colored halo.

Kirlian photography does not appear to have made any great impact in the Soviet Union, at least none of the official Soviet scientific bodies seem to have taken it very seriously. In the late 1960s, however, tales of astonishing psychical discoveries in Soviet-bloc countries began filtering into the West.

The interest of Soviet-bloc scientists in psychic phenomena has been grossly exaggerated in reports reaching the West. To read some books and articles, one might get the impression that there is a massive communist effort to develop psychical research, and that there is some sort of an international ESP race going on. Such an idea is simply unsupportable by the known facts. There is much less psychical research parapsychology, or call it what you will, going on in Russia and elsewhere in Eastern Europe than there is in the West. Communism with its materialistic philosophy is basically hostile to "spiritual" subjects like psychical research, and there is little in the way of funds or facilities available from private sources to carry on such research.

Still, as in the West, there are some individuals, including a few academically trained scientists, who are interested in such subjects and have done some work, most of it unofficial and all of it highly unsophisticated. Indeed, over the last few years Soviet psychical researchers have been hoaxed by tricksters whose sleight of hand would have fooled only the most gullible of Western parapsychologists.

Because communist-bloc psychical researchers are operating within a basically materialistic framework, they tend to

EXOTIC PSYCHIC PHENOMENA

give materialistic explanations to the alleged phenomena they observe. For example, some have spoken of a substance called "bioplasma," a theoretical fourth state of matter which flows out of living things and can be used to explain various sorts of psychic phenomena. This bioplasma is entirely hypothetical, and it reminds one of some of the materialistic explanations that nineteenth-century psychical researchers offered for the very same phenomena. They spoke of different kinds of "emanations" and "etheric fluids." Even earlier the mesmerists were talking about a "magnetic fluid" that connected all living things and was manipulated by the mesmerist. So the idea is not new, nor is there any more proof for it now than there was in the nineteenth or eighteenth centuries. But since the idea comes from Russia, and the terminology at least sounds "modern" and "scientific," it has been enthusiastically accepted by a lot of people who should know better.

Of all the experiments and phenomena reported from Eastern Europe, Kirlian photography is the one that has attracted the most attention. This is a bit surprising, for at first glance it appears as though Kirlian photography should be regarded as an electrical or photographic, rather than a psychic, phenomenon. The connection is that some people believe that Kirlian photographs show the body's bioplasma, or to use an older, more familiar term, the photographs show the human aura. The aura is some sort of an emanation of light and color that is supposed to surround all human beings, or according to some, all living things. This aura changes in color and shape in response to an individual's state of health, his character, mood, and spiritual nature. Some have even suggested that proper interpretation of the human aura can be used to predict a person's future.

The bright light said to radiate from the faces of some

saints was their aura, in the view of modern psychical theorists. The halo of gold that medieval painters placed around the heads of Jesus, Mary and the saints was, in this view, the human aura made visible. But under most circumstances, the human aura was visible only to seers, psychics or other "sensitives," and by no means to all of them or at all times.

Paracelsus, the great sixteenth-century alchemist and magician, talked about the aura this way: "The vital force is not enclosed in man, but radiates round him like a luminous sphere, and it may be made to act at a distance. In these semi-natural rays the imagination of man may produce healthy or morbid effects. It may poison the essence of life and cause diseases or it may purify it after it has been made impure, and restore health."

There was never any real agreement, even among occultists, as to exactly what the aura was supposed to be, what it showed, or who could see it and under what circumstances. The hope was that somehow technology would provide a method by which the invisible aura could be made visible to individuals without special psychic powers. There had been no lack of photographs of the aura in the past, but most of these were crude fakes. Even in a field where shoddy proof has occasionally gained wide acceptance, a picture with an obviously painted-in "halo" was going to deceive only the most stubbornly gullible. Most people were too sophisticated about photography to be taken in by that kind of fakery.

Then came the reports about Kirlian photography. When the Russian's techniques were adapted in the West, the pictures they produced looked very much like those of the aura so often described by sensitives. Hundreds and perhaps thousands of people throughout the United States are currently experimenting with some form of Kirlian photography. Much of the experimentation is basically of the basement workshop kind, in which individuals who may or may not know what they are doing work under uncontrolled conditions. But at least some of the experiments are being carried on by academically trained individuals working with adequate equipment.

One of the most active researchers in the field is UCLA psychologist Thelma Moss. She believes that Kirlian photography clearly demonstrates the human aura. Speaking to a reporter for *Time* magazine, she said, "We have done work with acupuncturists and [psychic] healers, and we find that the corona of the healer becomes intense before healing, and then afterward is more relaxed and less strong. We think we're looking at a transfer of energy from the healer to the injured person."

According to Sheila Ostrander and Lynn Schroeder, authors of the popular book *Psychic Discoveries Behind the Iron Curtain,* the Kirlians themselves believe that their process can detect changes in emotion and health, and would be a valuable diagnostic tool.

Do Kirlian photographs show the "human aura" or the mysterious bioplasma? Has an important diagnostic tool been discovered? The only honest answer to such questions is that no one really knows. Despite all the publicity, all the experimentation and all the theorizing, we know embarrassingly little about what Kirlian photographs are. The problem is that if one exposes a piece of film to high-frequency electronics, something will show up on the film. It would take a long series of careful experiments to find out whether this image can be related in any meaningful way to things such as health and emotions. Most of what passes for experimentation today consists of simply taking photographs by the Kirlian process or a reasonable facsimile and then imposing a meaning upon them afterwards. For example, a Kirlian photograph is taken of a man's hand. Sometime later another Kirlian photograph is taken of the same man's hand when he is ill. The photos look quite different, and the photographer proclaims that the difference is due to the state of health of the subject photographed. But is it, or are the differences between the two photographs due to entirely different causes?

Both high-frequency electronics and photography are extremely complicated subjects. The equipment for taking Kirlian photographs is sensitive to a variety of changes. The variation in the photographs might be due to a slightly different voltage, an alteration in the developing process, or any one of a dozen of other purely physical changes having nothing whatever to do with the state of the subject. Indeed, we have no idea what a "normal" Kirlian photograph is supposed to look like, and therefore it is impossible to know when one is "abnormal."

In addition, Kirlian photography is an area in which fakery is exceptionally easy, just because no one knows exactly what to look for in the first place.

Perhaps Kirlian photography will someday prove to be of great value in medicine, perhaps it will even finally make visible the eternally elusive "aura." But we don't know yet. There is no reason to let enthusiasm over the new technique cloud our judgment about the poor quality of the experimental evidence now available.

Some parapsychologists appear slightly embarrassed by all the publicity given to Kirlian photography. One told me that he regarded the excitement as part of an unfortunate tendency to "multiply mysteries" and find psychic significance in every unusual occurrence. He suspected that when all the information was in, Kirlian photography would turn out to be an artifact of the procedure rather than a picture of the human aura. He also feared that the adverse publicity might actually damage parapsychology's hard fight for scientific respectability.

A bit of cautionary history is instructive, for the reception given to Kirlian photography is not a new or unique event in the history of psychic investigation. Very often a new technique of any sort will be hailed as finally giving science a handle on the psychic. When photography itself was first developed, there were an enormous number of "spirit photographs" produced. These photographs were supposed to show "ghosts" or "spirits" not visible to the naked eye. Such photos were fakes, and to the eyes of observers today they seem so obviously fake that one wonders how anyone this side of a moron ever took them seriously. But it is unfair to judge past opinions by present standards. The heyday of spirit photography was the turn of the century, a time when most people were unsophisticated about the photographic process. The mere fact that pictures could be produced at all seemed quite wonderful. There was a feeling that "the camera doesn't quite lie," and therefore whatever appeared on film was somehow "true and real." This we now know is not the case. It was easy, even in the early days, to fake a photograph.

Deliberate fakery wasn't always necessary either. A number of perfectly honest people thought (and sometimes still think) that blurred or ghostly images and spots that appear in photographs are spirit images of some sort. They refuse to believe that these images are almost certainly due to some defect in the camera or film, and not to the influence of the spirits.

Kirlian photography may go the same way as the spirit photographs, and it would be extremely unwise to make any grandiose claims for it until a good deal more work is done.

Another area in which fascination with instrumentation seems to have run ahead of all good sense is the subject of the consciousness of plants.

For centuries people had toyed with the idea that plants possessed some sort of "vegetative soul," or more crudely, that they were inhabited by a variety of "nature spirit." Yet while these ideas were always around, they never played a large role in occult thinking, and they certainly never got into the mainstream of psychical investigation. Widespread interest in the consciousness of plants is, therefore, comparatively recent. It can be traced back to the mid-1960s and to the tales of how talking to plants improved their growth. The real "breakthrough," if it can be called that, came in 1966, when a polygraph, or lie detector, operator named Cleve Backster attached a galvanometer, the part of the polygraph used to measure the electrical resistance of the skin, to the leaf of a *dracaena*, a decorative plant that he happened to have in his office.

Backster wanted to see how the leaf was affected when the plant was watered. Electrical resistance is, as we have already pointed out, heavily influenced by the presence of water. The more water, the greater the conductivity. As the plant's roots sucked up water, Backster assumed that his instrument would show increased conductivity, but it didn't. Just the opposite happened.

The galvanometer readings from the leaf, as traced out by a pen on a piece of moving graph paper, looked to the polygraph operator like those of a human being experiencing some sort of temporary emotional stimulus. It was an interesting and unexpected observation. Backster rather playfully thought he might carry the experiment just a bit further. He dunked the leaf of the plant in a cup of hot coffee. No reaction. Perhaps he had not given it a strong enough "threat." So he decided that he would take some matches and burn one of the leaves. He never got a chance, for the moment he got the picture of a burning leaf clearly in his mind, the pen on the graph swept upward on the graph paper. The tracing it made, according to Backster, was very similar to that made by an individual who feels severely threatened. Not only had the plant reacted to a threat, it reacted to a threat that was completely mental. Backster's *dracaena* was not just conscious, it could read minds!

More tests followed. Backster found that he could get similar reactions from a leaf that had been detached from the plant, or even from a leaf that had been shredded and distributed between the electrodes of the galvanometer. Backster found that a plant leaf appeared to react to the moves made by a spider in the room that was trying to escape being captured by a human being, and that the plant reacted before the spider actually made its move—in short, the plant was able to read the spiders mind!

Oddly, though, plants didn't usually react to one another. "The last thing a plant expects is another plant to give it trouble. So long as there is animal life around, they seem to be attuned to animal life. Animals and people are mobile and could need careful monitoring," says Backster.

Plants, in Backster's view, are very emotional. When they become overtaxed, they play possum or faint. One day Backster was planning to demonstrate his monitoring technique to a visiting plant physiologist. He hooked his polygraph up to a plant leaf, but got no reaction whatsoever. A second plant showed no response, nor did a third or a fourth. Finally Backster asked the physiologist whether his work involved harming plants. "Yes," the physiologist replied. "I terminate the plants I work with. I put them in an oven and roast them to obtain their dry weight for my analysis." Only after the physiologist left did Backster's plants again begin to show "normal" reactions, and he concluded that they had simply "passed out" when brought face to face with a mass murderer.

To the uninitiated all this may sound just a bit silly. But Backster is not the only person in America today hooking up plants to a variety of instruments and getting reactions that one normally would assume were limited to conscious creatures. Backster's work and similar experiments and theories by a host of others were collected together in a volume entitled *The Secret Life of Plants* written by Peter Tompkins and Christopher Bird. The book became an unexpected best seller in early 1974. The enormous popularity of such a book tells us a great deal about the current interests of the American public. But first let's look at the basic question posed by the experiments of Backster and others. Do plants have a consciousness?

The kindest answer one can reasonably make is, perhaps they do, but neither the experiments of Cleve Backster nor any of the other experimental work cited in *The Secret Life of Plants* proves anything. As with Kirlian photography, one can't be sure whether the results come from the subject (in this case the plants) or are due to some peculiarity in the equipment, the procedure, or the experimenter himself. Put on rubber boots, change the humidity of a room, forget to clean the electrical terminals of the machine and you will change the readings. If you credit a plant with reading your mind, how can you be sure of the exact moment a thought came into your mind? Did the plant react when you were thinking about something, when you first thought of it, or after the thought was firmly and clearly in your mind? Data of this sort is open to the widest range of interpretation. And then there is always the possibility that some of the data is just plain faked.

Though the procedure sounds simple when related by Tompkins and Bird, the problems involved in testing plants with instruments designed for human beings are really enormously complex. Even assuming that the experimenter's equipment is working properly, and that the data received is correctly and honestly reported (a large assumption indeed), how can we be sure that the readings mean what people like Backster say they mean? If plants really did have emotions, would they necessarily register on a polygraph in the same way as human emotions do?

If plants can read minds, why can't they do something with the information they obtain? If the grass on your lawn knows when you are about to mow, it should be able to try to escape somehow, otherwise what is the point of knowing what is going to happen? One of the primary rules of evolutionary theory is that structures and faculties do not exist for their own sake; they must serve some function that contributes to the survival of the species.

It's pointless and rather ridiculous to press a scientific argument against the plant consciousness theory too far, because nothing produced by the plant consciousness people to date bears more than the most superficial resemblance to scientific procedure. Even within the astonishingly loose procedures that they allow themselves, the plant consciousness supporters can find ready excuses when their plants fail to perform as expected. If a plant does not react, it has "fainted."

Some of the arguments put forth by the supporters of plant consciousness go to the very core of the dispute between orthodox and unorthodox science. Marcel Vogel, another person who works with plants and polygraphs, is quoted by Tompkins and Bird as saying:

"Hundreds of laboratory workers around the world are going to be frustrated and disappointed . . . until they realize that empathy between plant and human is the key, and learn how to establish it. No amount of checking in laboratories is going to prove a thing until the experiments are done by properly trained observers. Spiritual development is indispensable. But this runs counter to the philosophy of many scientists, who do not realize that creative experimentation means that the experimenters must become part of their experiments."

The response to this attitude, that is held not only by Vogel but common to many others who have worked with psychic subjects, was given by plant physiologist Arthur W. Galston in *Natural History* magazine:

"What do you want to believe? Results that are obtained when carefully described experiments are repeated by competent investigators anywhere in the world? Or results that can be obtained only by a select few in 'special contact' with their test material? Scientists are well acquainted with results that occur only occasionally. They have learned that under such circumstances it is easy to fool yourself into thinking you have obtained a positive result, when all that has really happened is that a random variation, either in biological material or experimental conditions, has cropped up ... It is also axiomatic among scientists not to really trust any results that have been reported successful in only one laboratory. Published results must describe the experiments and organisms in such detail that conscientious researchers elsewhere can get approximately the same results."

Since the tests themselves are without any real merit and the conclusions often laughable, why has the subject attracted so much attention? Part of the answer lies in our fascination with, and faith in, machines. The polygraph has wires and dials and it produces a visible record of jagged lines on a piece of paper. These records somehow appear to be "scientific proof."

Most people fail to realize that the lie detector, even when used properly on human beings, is an instrument of questionable value. When used on plants under uncontrolled conditions, the tracings are not a proven record of emotional changes; they are merely jagged lines, which may or may not have a relationship to something happening within the plant. The supporters of plant consciousness have fallen for the cult of "scientism," where complicated gadgetry replaces carefully constructed experiments and clear thinking. It somehow reminds one of those old horror movies where the mad scientist's laboratory is filled with glass tubes, bubbling flasks and electrostatic generators sparking away, or newer movies where this paraphernalia is replaced by a big computer console. None of the gadgetry has any meaning; it's just there to make the background look "scientific."

Yet there are plenty of foolish ideas presented in scientific-looking formats every year, so why has this particular one caught on? There is obviously the eternal appeal of the weird and the strange, and these ideas are unquestionably weird and strange. More significantly, though, plant consciousness seems to lend new credence to the ancient idea of a conscious universe in which all things—animal, vegetable and mineral—are somehow interconnected. This is the sort of thinking that in past ages led to practices like astrology, alchemy and high magic.

The belief in a conscious interrelated universe is not an unsophisticated one. Nor is it necessarily wrong. It is merely unprovable at present. Hooking up house plants to lie dectectors isn't really getting us any closer to the basic secrets of the universe, either.

More conventional—if anything in this field can truly be called conventional—is an enormous upsurge in interest in Out of the Body Experiences. The term is used so frequently now that for convenience it is abbreviated OOBE. What is an out-of-the-body experience? It is a phrase best defined by example. Here is a typical one cited in the book *Psychical Phenomena and the Physical World* by Charles McCreery:

". . . It was summer time, the day bright and sunny and I wore a dress and blazer. I was walking along Brentwood High Street in Essex and there were people shopping and walking near me. As far as I can remember I was thinking of nothing in particular when suddenly I was about 15 ft. above myself and I watched myself walking towards a cinema called the Palace which was a short distance ahead of me. I noticed the people walking round me. I suppose I watched myself walk about 30 to 40 steps and then I was back 'inside' myself again. I felt in no way different and just went on walking along the High Street. The whole incident must have taken a few seconds . . ."

This is a fairly mundane sort of OOBE. The individual was only fifteen feet removed from herself, and the entire experience lasted just a few seconds. Many OOBE's are much more dramatic. McCreery quotes another experience in which a woman was in a motorcycle accident, and recalled observing her own body on the road and people running toward her shouting, "She's dead!"

"And then a feeling (I can still feel the awful shock of this whenever I recall the incident) of terrible fear came over me. I knew I HAD to return to my body before it was touched. There was a dreadful sense of urgency, or it would be too late. It is this sensation of dread that remains so indelible.

"I went back and lay down on top of myself. And as I did so I felt the hardness of the road beneath me and all the terrible pains of brusiing lacerations and concussion that I was subsequently found to be suffering from . . .

"I was moving about thinking I was my normal body . . . Everything looked normal . . . my 'floating self' behaved exactly as my physical. . . ."

Other OOBEs apparently concern travel over long distances, where an individual may feel that he is far out of sight of his own physical body, and that he is present at a scene many miles away. The border between this type of an experience and clairvoyance, where an individual believes he is perceiving a distant event, is not a well-defined one. The principal difference is that in clairvoyance the individual does not feel that he has left his physical body, but rather that the distant event has somehow come into his mind. In an OOBE the individual feels that he is actually an observer at the distant event. Since many of these experiences take place while dreaming and are incompletely remembered, parapsychologists are often unsure as to whether to classify them as clairvoyance or OOBE.

There have been few scientific surveys of the matter, but OOBEs may be quite common, particularly the ones in which the individual feels momentarily a short distance outside of his own body. When a group of 155 college students were asked if they had experienced the feeling of being outside of their bodies, 30 percent said they had. When I was young, I had several OOBEs. (The only "paranormal" experience I can ever recall having.) I would lie in bed and feel "myself" floating up toward the ceiling, then I could look down and see my body still on the bed. Many others that I have talked to have had similar experiences. They seem as common as the feeling of *déjà vu,* and like *déjà vu,* many who experience such feelings are not inclined to regard them as being in any way paranormal.

Are they? During OOBEs does the soul, or spirit, or something actually leave the physical body, or are they the results of dreams, hallucinations, or some strange but entirely material sensory quirk? For my part I had always believed that the feeling of floating up toward the ceiling was either part of a dream or a pre-sleep reverie. I never thought there was anything paranormal about the feeling until I began hearing of OOBEs.

So long as OOBEs remained a spontaneous and uncontrolled event, there seemed little chance that anyone was going to learn any more about them. But recently there has been an attempt to bring this phenomenon into the laboratory.

While many people believe that they have experienced OOBEs, a few people claim to have experienced them regularly, and even believe that they can control such experiences. Some mystics have reported developing the ability for out-of-the-body travel, or astral projection, as it is commonly called, to a high degree.

One of the few humorous accounts of astral projection was given by Anne Osmont, a French occultist and journalist who died in 1953. Mlle Osmont described her talent for astral travel to a couple that she knew, but the wife, whose name was Annie, was skeptical. So Mlle Osmont decided to prove her wrong.

That very night she projected her astral body to her friends' flat. They were both asleep and she took note of the color and style of their nightclothes. But she felt that would be poor proof of her visit. She then decided to leave some physical evidence of her presence by knocking something over. Her attention fixed on a small liqueur glass on the mantelpiece. Moving it was exceedingly difficult (tales of moving physical objects while in the astral body are very rare). Finally, though, she managed to push it over, and it smashed on the floor.

The couple woke up, and Annie said angrily, "I bet it's that imbecile Osmont!" On her next ordinary visit she first saw the husband and repeated Annie's words to him. He said that his wife had been very angry, because the goblet had been a family heirloom.

Some experienced astral travelers have even expressed fears that one day they would project themselves so far out of their body that they would be unable to return, or they would be gone so long that their friends would assume they were dead, and bury their physical body, or even that they might somehow sustain an injury from the shock of reentering their own body.

One turn-of-the-century adept at astral projection was Sylvan Muldoon. He recorded, "When returning to the body, the greater the speed and the greater the distance, the more forceful will be the jolt. Velocity and distance combined produce the maximum repercussion; but speed is the most important of the two; for even at a distance of separation of only one foot, if the return to the physical is with intense velocity, the physical will undergo a violent shock."

In the late 1960s Dr. Charles T. Tart of the University of California at Davis met a man (referred to in the literature only as Mr. X) who claimed to have experienced hundreds of OOBEs. Since most of Mr. X's experiences had taken place while sleeping, Tart arranged a test under standard dream laboratory conditions. The aim was twofold. The primary purpose was to test the reality of the OOBE. A five-digit random number written on a piece of cardboard was placed on a high shelf in the equipment room next to where Mr. X was to sleep. He was instructed to try to float up to the shelf during his time out of the body, and then look at the number and memorize it so that he could report it the next day. The second aim of the test was to monitor what changes, if any, took place in Mr. X's body and brain functions during an OOBE.

The plan seemed a good one, but it never really got going, because Mr. X had a hard time sleeping at all with the electrodes attached to his head. On only one night during the experimental period did Mr. X report having OOBEs. The recollection of the technician who monitored the experimental equipment was contained in an article Dr. Tart wrote for the *International Journal of Parapsychology:*

"Patient feels he succeeded in the experiment; in the first [period of sleep] he saw two men and one woman seated somewhere in the hospital—he pinched them. In the second [period of sleep] the patient saw me and he said I had a visitor, which I did. However, it is possible that Mr. X may have heard the visitor cough . . . Mr. X states that he patted the visitor on the cheeks and tried to take his hand but that the visitor avoided [him]. Mr. X recalls that he left the cot, went under it and out the door into the recording room and then into the hallway . . . the patient did not see the number."

It all could have been a dream, completely made up, or it could have been a real out of the body experience. There is no way of deciding from the available evidence. Another subject, a Miss Z, was able to report the five-digit number successfully after a number of unsuccessful attempts, but Dr. Tart hesitated to make any startling claims for this modest success. "Sensory leakage," deliberate or accidental, is always a strong possibility in a single case. A large number of successful experiments of this type would have to be carried out before one could conclude that there was indeed something to the feeling of out of the body experiences.

It appears that there is a lot happening in the psychic world of the seventies, but the key problem, of whether the variety of psi experiences take place at all, remains as tantalizingly elusive as ever.

7
ALTERED STATES OF CONSCIOUSNESS

WHEN Captain Edgar Mitchell returned from outer space, he said that during the trip he had experienced an "altered state of consciousness." So going to the moon is apparently one way of altering consciousness. It is not a technique that is likely to be practical for most of us. But there are other methods—hundreds of them. Everything from drinking to long-distance running has been tried. Sensory deprivation is thought to be an excellent method of altering consciousness; so is sensory overload.

The Book of Highs, by Edward Rosenfeld, is advertised as "A whole consciousness catalog—250 ways to alter your consciousness without drugs." Some of the suggested highs are nearly as impractical as space travel (which is also listed). Take, for example, high number 214, kayak disease. Says the author, "Next time you're in Greenland, if you go out hunting in a kayak and you stay out for more than three days, well, that's usually when kayak disease sets in. Terrible hallucinations, both auditory and visual, may affect you; extreme disorientation may also ensue. Be careful." Other suggestions like bouncing on a trampoline may not really alter consciousness in any significant way. Still the variety of techniques by which altered states of consciousness can be attained is impressive. And that is leaving aside drugs, the most powerful method of altering consciousness.

It was the interest in psychedelic drugs which began in the late 1950s and early 1960s that sparked current fascination with altered states of consciousness, or ASCs, as they are now familiarly known. When the drugs failed to produce the expected millennium, much of the luster disappeared from the drug scene. But the desire to alter consciousness, this time without drugs, remained and continues to grow to this day.

Moreover the subject of ASCs has become increasingly interesting to orthodox scientists. Over the last few years there have been a number of very respectable scientific conferences on the subject, and reports in the journals have proliferated. Despite the accumulation of data, we are still not really sure what an ASC or being "high" is, what it means, or why so many people appear to want to get that way.

In this region psychical researchers should have a long lead on their more orthodox colleagues. They are more comfortable with strange ideas and have always suspected that the key to the new view of reality that they seek might lie in the study of other forms of consciousness. For many years they have taken the subject of ASCs very seriously, whereas orthodox scientists have tried to "explain away" such states as "abnormal." The entranced medium who supposedly is in touch with the spirits of the dead is in an altered state of consciousness. The clairvoyant or seer who reports on a distant or future event is generally assumed to have received this vision while in an altered state of consciousness. We already noted that the most vigorous and ingenious extrasensory perception research going on today concerns our most familiar altered state of consciousness—sleep.

In the early days of psychical research there was a genuine hope that mesmerism, magnetism or hypnotism would yield the secrets of the psychic world. Hypnosis seemed promising for several reasons—first, it was controllable, unlike the spontaneous psi event or the often suspicious trances of professional mediums; second, because hypnotic subjects regularly reported experiencing unique and perhaps psychic phenomena. Historically, interest in hypnotism and the phenomena it produced prepared the way for the development of organized psychical research.

Franz Mesmer's most important disciple was the Marquis de Puysegur. It was Puysegur who first actually put hypnotic subjects to sleep. Mesmer sent his patients into screaming twitching fits or convulsions, but Puysegur disliked the violence and found the "magnetic cure" worked just as well when patients were in a relaxed and sleep-like state. He coined the term somnambulist, or artificial sleepwalker. While Puysegur's subjects were in a somnambulistic state, he discovered that he could control their actions by voice commands or by simply thinking. Puysegur attributed this mental control to Mesmer's theoretical magnetic fluid, but today we would call the same sort of control evidence of telepathy.

Magnetists or hypnotists, as they were soon to be called, regularly reported establishing a state of "rapport" with their subjects. This rapport allowed the hypnotist to sit in his own house and simply "will" his distant subject to go to sleep or get up or do any of a number of things. Other hypnotists said that their subjects experienced episodes of clairvoyance or had the ability to pick out different colors of wool with their fingertips alone. Many individuals claimed that while in a hypnotic trance they possessed the ability to diagnose or heal sickness. Hypnotists were also credited with the ability to cause sickness at a distance. Mary Baker Eddy, the founder of Christian Science, attributed much of the world's serious illness to the actions of "evil mesmerists," and even she was terrified of their power.

Hypnotists also found that their subjects began to converse with the spirits of the dead. Frank Podmore, a historian of psychical research and hypnosis, wrote: "When table-turning and spirit-rapping were introduced into England from America, the mesmerists soon identified the mysterious force which caused the phenomena with the mesmeric or neuro-vital fluid. A little later, when the trance and its manifestations were exploited in the interests of the new gospel of Spiritualism, many of the English mesmerists, who had been prepared by the utterances of their own clairvoyants for some such development, proclaimed themselves adherents of the new faith."

One of the primary aims announced by the Society for Psychical Research when it was founded in 1882 was to investigate the claims made for hypnotism. A typical investigation of hypnotic rapport was conducted by psychical research pioneer Edmund Gurney. The hypnotist was George Albert Smith, and the subject a man named Conway. Conway was put into a "tolerably deep trance." Smith and Gurney stood behind the entranced Conway without touching him. First Gurney pinched Smith's right arm, and Conway reacted by rubbing his own right arm at the exact same spot. When Gurney pinched Smith's left arm, Conway rubbed his left arm and complained loudly of the pain.

Smith was then given a number of substances to taste, and Conway responded appropriately. When Smith put some hot cayenne pepper into his mouth, Conway shouted, "Oh! You call it good, do you? Oh, give us something to rinse that down. Draws your mouth in all manner of shapes. Bitter and acid, frightful. You've got some cayenne down my throat, I know." He then asked for water.

There is an enormous quantity of similar material, but it is hard to decide what it all proves or if it proves anything. The early reports from mesmerists are entirely anecdotal, and suffer from all the limitations of that type of evidence. The initial SPR investigations, while more carefully regulated and reported, are also open to a great deal of criticism. For example, Smith was one of the star subjects in a huge number of early SPR experiments. He seemed so talented that he was actually hired by the Society, and at his direction a number of other subjects like Conway were brought in. Some years after these initial experiments one of Smith's early associates, Douglas Blackburn, announced that he and Smith had fooled the SPR investigators by using some rather simple tricks. Smith denied the charge, but Blackburn built a convincing case. Smith had been a semi-professional magician, and after his work with the SPR he went into the carnival business. As a result a cloud of suspicion hangs over all of the experiments he carried out with the SPR, including those involving hypnosis. It would have been easy enough for Smith to signal the supposedly entranced Conway, for Edmund Gurney was not a particularly skeptical observer.

During the first half of the twentieth century hypnosis began to shed much of the aura of the mysterious and supernatural that had once surrounded it. It became almost respectable. The use of hypnosis to replace mild anesthesia in both surgery and dentistry became commonplace. Nothing dissipates an aura of mystery faster than an association with dentistry.

Stripped of its exotic trappings, the light hypnotic trance can be a rather disappointing experience. Some years ago I discovered that I was an excellent subject for hypnosis. The discovery was a bit of a shock, since I had always unconsciously assumed that persons who were easily hypnotized had a "weak will." There were about ten of us being given a test for hypnotic susceptibility. We were told to put our clasped hands above our heads. The hypnotist then said that he would count to three and ask us to pull our hands apart, but we would not be able to unlock our fingers. He counted to three and the nine others easily dropped their hands to their sides while I continued to struggle with fingers that refused somehow to unlock.

When I was actually hypnotized, I went under in what I was later told was near record time. The trouble is that I never really felt that I was "under" or that anything unusual had happened to me. I was perfectly aware of my surroundings, there were no time or space distortions, and I later remembered everything that had happened to me when I was in a "trance." The hypnotist made a number of suggestions which I felt I could have easily disobeyed if I had wanted to. But I just didn't want to disobey. I felt that it would be simpler to go along. So I did everything he asked. I wasn't asked to do anything particularly bizarre, so I really don't know if some sort of an internal censor would have stopped me or not. But when I came out of the "trance," I was quite sure that I had never been in one. I thought I had just been going along with the joke. Only later when I talked to other people who had been hypnotized did I realize that we had all experienced the same thing and that the desire to just "go along" was the essence of being hypnotized.

Some scientists have said that there really is no separate and distinct state of consciousness that can be called a "hypnotic trance" or "hypnotic state," that rather hypnotism induces a condition of heightened suggestibility in the subject

ALTERED STATES OF CONSCIOUSNESS 143

—nothing more. Interestingly the EEG of hypnotized subjects is no different from that of normal waking subjects. According to most studies, people in deep hypnotic trances show abundant alpha waves when they are sitting calmly with their eyes shut, and predominant beta activity when their eyes are open and they are performing specific tasks suggested by the hypnotist. Measurements of other physical functions also indicate that the hypnotized person reacts in almost exactly the same manner as the waking person. This is in marked contrast to findings about subjects in a state of meditation where the differences from the waking state are easily measurable.

The importance of hypnosis to psychical research has diminished considerably since the early days, but it has by no means disappeared. Some parapsychologists use hypnosis in order to try to help promising subjects develop their ESP abilities, in much the same way as some trainers have attempted to use hypnosis to improve the performance of certain athletes—by relaxing them and increasing their confidence. Both relaxation and confidence are generally considered important to a good psychic's performance, just as they are to athletic performance.

The prime modern exponent of hypnosis for training sensitives is Dr. Milan Ryzl, formerly of Prague, Czechoslovakia, and now of California. The best advertisement for Dr. Ryzl's hypnotic training methods is Pavel Stepanek, the only psychic to make the *Guinness Book of World Records.* He is called "The highest consistent performer in tests to detect powers of extrasensory perception." Stepanek's record is based on a series of tests in which he was supposed to pick a green card or a white card in a sealed envelope. The long series of tests ran from May, 1967, to March, 1968, and the odds against Stepanek's score being pure chance were estimated at more than 100 octillion to one.

Stepanek is one of the very few well-known sensitives who does not resent the tediousness of taking the same test over and over again. Indeed Stepanek seems to positively enjoy sorting out sealed envelopes, because it is the only psychic ability that he has. He's no better than anyone else at other sorts of card guessing tests. Still Stepanek's ability to perform this one feat with near miraculous results should provide the sort of final conclusive proof of extrasensory abilities that parapsychologists have long sought.

As seems inevitable in parapsychology, however, dissident voices have been raised. Critics claim that Stepanek's high scores are not due to his clairvoyant ability to see through sealed envelopes, but his perfectly normal ability to feel through them. The different colored cards used to test the sensitive, the critics claim, bend almost imperceptibly in different directions and that it is the slight bend that tips Stepanek off as to which color card is in the envelope. When a Scottish psychologist traveled to Prague to test Stepanek, he brought his own cards made of plastic. These were perfectly flat, and Stepanek could do nothing with them. An off day, say Stepanek supporters; no one can perform 100 percent all the time. Perhaps so, but some suspicion is justified.

A more spectacular use of hypnosis in the psychic field is age regression. Hypnosis has long been used by psychiatrists to help their patients remember, and in a sense relive, forgotten or repressed incidents from years past. The next logical step is to find out whether the hypnotic subject can recall incidents from past lives. The step is logical, of course, only if one believes in reincarnation, but this doctrine has always had a solid core of supporters in the West, and interest in it appears to be growing.

The first well-documented case of age regression through

hypnosis was presented by a European psychologist named T. Flournoy in the 1900s. His subject was a young Swiss woman whom he gave the pseudonym Hélène Smith. Miss Smith had been an amateur medium who gave frequent séances for her friends and easily slipped into a trance. Under hypnosis she revealed that in a previous incarnation she had been Marie Antoinette. Before that she had been the daughter of an Arab sheik and an Indian princess named Simandini. But her crowning achievement came when she recalled a previous life on the planet Mars. She even drew pictures of the Martian landscape and wrote in what she said was Martian language.

Today when people speak quite casually of visitors from outer space, Miss Smith's tale would be almost commonplace in the psychic world. But at the turn of the century it was a sensation and Professor Flournoy's book on the case entitled *From India to the Planet Mars* was a best seller of sorts.

But alas, this wonderful tale was too good to be true. Miss Smith's Martian drawings were pedestrian, and in no way resembled what we now know of the Martian landscape. The "Martian language" was clearly based on French, her own native language, and she had even been observed visiting the Oriental section of the Geneva public library, where she could easily have picked up the few authentic bits of Arabic and Indian history that appeared in her "age regression." Despite all this, Hélène Smith found a wealthy American patron and was able to spend the rest of her current life plunging ever deeper into her past lives.

The best-known modern case of age regression is that of "Bridey Murphy," which burst upon the scene in 1956. This sensation began when a Pueblo, Colorado, businessman and amateur hypnotist named Morey Bernstein took one of his subjects, a woman he called Ruth Simmons, on an "age regression." Under hypnosis Mrs. Simmons spoke of her past life as Bridey Murphy, who lived in nineteenth-century Ireland.

Popular occult and psychic literature contains scores of similar cases which receive little attention, but Bridey Murphy caught on and for about six months all America was very Bridey Murphy conscious. The publicity had one good effect —it gave skeptical reporters a chance to thoroughly check out the facts, something that the true believer rarely has time or inclination to do. The reporters could find no trace of a real Bridey Murphy in the Irish records. They did notice, though, that the hypnotized subject's descriptions of life in nineteenth-century Ireland contained a distressingly large number of anachronisms and errors. The crusher came when a Chicago newspaper discovered that Mrs. Simmons, who grew up in Chicago, had lived across the street from an Irishwoman named Mrs. Anthony Corkell. Mrs. Corkell's maiden name was Bridie Murphy. Mrs. Simmons said she could not recall Bridie Murphy Corkell, but the public was fed up by that time.

The collapse of the Bridey Murphy boom made the whole subject of age regression through hypnosis a rather sensitive one for psychical researchers. Though few of them had actually endorsed the claims made for Bridey Murphy, and some had actually tried to warn the public of what might happen, it still gave the whole psychic field a black eye. Even today, nearly twenty years after Bridey Murphy, psychical researchers are very wary of such tales. And in truth they should be. Hypnosis is an extremely tricky technique to work with. Neither the case of Bridey Murphy nor even the more extreme case of Hélène Smith necessarily involved deliberate fraud on the part of either the hypnotist or subject. There is a general assumption that the hypnotic subject will always tell the truth when asked, but this isn't so. The hypnotic subject will try to be agreeable to the wishes of the hypnotist. If the hypnotist wants stories about past lives, then the subject will obligingly supply him with such stories.

In their book *Psychic Discoveries Behind the Iron Curtain*, Sheila Ostrander and Lynn Schroeder introduce a certain amount of confusion into the subject of hypnotic age regression in a discussion of what they label "artificial reincarnation."

There is a description of a scene in a large studio filled with art students. The instructor, Dr. Vladimir L. Raikov, enters the room with a visitor. He introduces the visitor to one of the students, a young girl in her early twenties, who stands up and announces, "I am Raphael of Urbino."

The account continues, "The visitor wasn't as surprised at the name as he was at the nonchalant way this seemingly normal, wide-awake girl tried to pass herself off as the great Renaissance painter.

" 'Could you tell me, by any chance, what year it is?' he asked.

" 'Why, 1505, of course.' "

The girl denied all knowledge of developments like cameras, jet planes and space satellites, and became quite annoyed when the visitor tried to press the subject. " 'Phantasmagoria! It's all foolishness. You're bothering me with this nonsense!' the girl cried angrily."

But there was nothing of Bridey Murphy about this female Russian Raphael. She was no different than three other "Raphaels" in the same class. They had all been hypnotized by Dr. Raikov into thinking they were the sixteenth-century Italian master. Despite the rather exotic title "artificial reincarnation," this appears to be more of an unorthodox training method than an attempt at "age regression."

Another technique for altering consciousness used by modern psychical researchers goes back a long way. One of the gentler methods employed by medieval inquisitors for getting confessions out of accused witches was placing them in a bag, tying the bag to a tree, and then swinging the bag back and forth for hours. Eventually being sealed inside of the swinging bag produced panic, and led to a confession.

But the process also tended to induce hallucinations and visions. Some believe that the witches themselves adapted the method, as a means of stimulating the hallucinations that would "carry" them to their sabbat. This device got the name "witches' cradle."

The power of the witches' cradle to inspire panic and hallucinations comes from the fact that the subject is in a state of mild sensory deprivation. He cannot see what is going on, or hear very well, and the swinging back and forth confuses one's sense of balance, motion and touch.

Psychologists became very interested in exploring the effects of sensory deprivation (or sensory dep, as it has come to be known) during the early 1960s. Subjects wearing eye-shields, ear baffles and thick gloves were confined for hours in tiny temperature-controlled rooms. Cut off from normal sensory input they, like the witches in the bag, often panicked, sometimes after a mere twenty minutes. But those who stuck with it began to experience strange dream-like states, and often vivid hallucinations.

To experience a limited amount of sensory dep *The Book of Highs* recommends that you put on a blindfold and ear baffles and shut yourself up in a pillow-filled closet. You are not supposed to be disturbed, but the book warns that help *must* always be available. "Enter the closet and do your best to limit all movements, even twitching and scratching. Don't stay in too long! Usually a couple of hours will produce

ALTERED STATES OF CONSCIOUSNESS 149

effects that are both inescapable and dominant."

The recent history of experience with sensory dep points up something very important about altered states of consciousness. The quality and content of the ASC experience is heavily influenced by the expectations of the subject. At first many people found sensory dep unbearable, but researchers now report that the majority of subjects find it relaxing and pleasurable. The people who are climbing into pillow-filled closets are seeking pleasant highs.

Dr. John C. Lilly, the man who became famous for "talking to dolphins," developed a great interest in altered states of consciousness, and his experiments with sensory deprivation, in which he was the subject, are still classics. Because of his work with sea creatures, Lilly had a large water tank at his disposal. He heated the water in the tank to 93 degrees, a temperature which he found was neither hot nor cold. Fitted up with a variety of rubber pads so that his legs would not sink, and breathing through air tubes attached to his padded head mask, Lilly suspended himself in the middle of this warm, womb-like tank for hours on end. He did not find the experience an unpleasant one, but after a while strange things began to happen. Writes Lilly in his book *The Center of the Cyclone:*

"I went through experiences in which other people apparently joined me in this dark silent environment. I could actually see them, feel them, and hear them. At other times, I went through dreamlike sequences, waking dreams as they are now called, in which I watched what was happening. At other times I apparently tuned in on networks of communication that are normal below our levels of awareness, networks of civilizations way beyond ours. I did hours of work on my own hindrances to understanding myself, on my life situation. I did hours of meditation, concentration, and contemplation, without knowing that this was what I was doing. It was only later in reading the literature that I found that the states I was getting into resembled those attained by other techniques."

Later Lilly used LSD in conjunction with his tank experiments, and reported even stranger experiences. He describes out-of-the-body trips into outer space, and (though the terms seem contradictory) through the interior of his own body. He also tells of meeting two beings (or something) that he calls guides. The guides advised him about what he should do in the future.

Experiences such as those described by Dr. John Lilly are fascinating, but they are also unsatisfactory, for we cannot hope to share them, nor is there any way that we can objectively "measure" the experience. We can either accept the description of the experience as valid and meaningful or reject it.

But there is another way in which sensory deprivation can be employed in an attempt to test the reality of psychic events. We have already mentioned the theory that most psychic impressions are lost to us because they are overwhelmed by the tremendous number and strength of the sensory impressions that assail us at all times. Moments of restful quiet or sleep are the times in which people are most likely to report spontaneous psychic experiences.

At Maimonides Hospital, where so much work on extrasensory perception and dreaming has been done, parapsychologists have also conducted a modest number of experiments in which the subjects are in a state of sensory dep. The aim is not to send the subject into far-out states like those described by Dr. Lilly, but rather to see whether an individual deprived of normal sensory input is more receptive to telepathic images than he would be in a state of normal

ALTERED STATES OF CONSCIOUSNESS

waking consciousness.

The setup of such experiments is much the same as it is for dream studies. An agent tries to "send" a target picture to a percipient who is in sensory dep. The Maimonides researchers have used a number of different sensory deprivation techniques. The most common is simply putting the subject in a quiet room wearing the padded halves of ping pong balls over his eyes and earphones through which is fed a static-like "white" noise.

The Maimonides experimenters have also tried variations on the witches' cradle. In one designed by Dr. Harry Hermon of the Maimonides staff, the blindfolded subject trussed up in a harness is swung gently from the ceiling. A similar effect is produced by ASCID, the Altered States of Consciousness Induction Device designed by Robert Masters and Jean Houston of the Foundation for Mind Research, a group that has also cooperated in some of the Maimonides dream studies.

In the ASCID the blindfolded subject is strapped upright onto a metal frame attached to a larger rigid support structure. The frame swings gently back and forth, and left and right. There is also a horizontal model of ASCID available. While in the device the subject looks as though he is undergoing some ancient torture, though the experience is said to be not an unpleasant one, and is often compared to the sensation of being rocked as a child.

How well do subjects in a state of sensory deprivation score on ESP tests? According to Charles Honorton, a senior research associate at Maimonides, they do pretty well. Out of thirty subjects in a state of mild sensory deprivation, 43 percent scored "hits"—they picked the correct set of pictures. Since they were given a choice of four sets of pictures, 25 percent hits is what one would expect from pure chance.

Honorton told *The New York Times* that the odds against such a score occurring randomly are 1 in 50—not astronomical odds, by any means, but in a class with what are considered good scores on standard ESP tests.

A slightly different scoring system was used on thirty subjects tested in a witches' cradle. There were six choices of pictures, and if the subject chose the target among the first three, then the trial was counted as a "hit." According to Honorton, the rate of success on this test was 63 percent, when 50 percent would have been the chance expectation. There was a considerable difference in scores between those subjects who said they had focused their attention inwardly, rather than toward their surroundings. The inward-looking subjects got a 76 percent hit rate, while those whose attention was directed outward toward their environment had only a 46 percent rate.

It would be foolish in the extreme to try to draw any broad conclusions from these very limited tests. We know that sensory deprivation is a powerful technique for producing altered states of consciousness, and that the subject in sensory dep often experiences novel and very powerful sensations. The significance of such perceptions is unclear and likely to remain so for some time to come.

In the more mundane area of trying to find out if sensory dep improves ESP scores, the first tentative studies are intriguing, but nothing more. Not even the most enthusiastic supporters of the ESP thesis would claim that the scores obtained on tests so far are any more than marginally significant. A large number of tests under a variety of controls will have to be conducted. Whatever else it might finally prove, sensory dep is apparently not going to provide the sort of fast and conclusive proof that has evaded psychical researchers for nearly a century.

ALTERED STATES OF CONSCIOUSNESS 153

Finally we come to drugs. Psychoactive drugs are really responsible for the ASC boom in the first place. The amount of material that has been written on psychoactive drugs and the drug phenomena over the last ten years is staggering. And drug taking is hardly a new experience for mankind; it goes back to antiquity. It would be hopeless to attempt to tackle such a huge subject in just a few pages. And, as with other altered states of consciousness, there is not really a great deal we can do with the internal quality of the experience. Nor does measuring the blood pressure, heart rate, or even the brain waves of an individual who has taken psychoactive drugs tell us very much.

In ancient Greece the Oracle of Delphi chewed laurel leaves to induce a prophetic trance. Tribal wizards have often taken drugs before issuing prophecies. In recent years many drug users have claimed to have orthodox (if such a word is permissible in this context) psychic experiences under the influence of drugs—that is, they experienced spontaneous telepathy, clairvoyance and precognition. A few professional psychics have claimed that drugs have enhanced their natural abilities.

It would seem that drug-induced psychic phenomena would be a natural area of investigation for the parapsychologist. Yet a surprisingly small amount of work has actually been done. Around the turn of the century, William James experimented with peyote and nitrous oxide, popularly known as laughing gas, using himself as the subject. One of the things James wanted to find out was whether the substances might induce psychic powers, for though he was very interested in them, James felt that he had none under normal circumstances. Neither the peyote nor the laughing gas improved James's psychic abilities.

In the 1930s J. B. Rhine gave some of his card guessing

subjects mild sedatives or stimulants to see if the drugs improved their ESP scores. The sedatives appeared to reduce scores very slightly, while the stimulants raised them slightly. The results, however, were too meager to be conclusive.

Users of powerful psychedelic drugs like LSD claimed fantastic psychic experiences—from precognition to a mystical rapport where members of a group all shared thoughts, and age regressions in which under the influence of drugs they recalled past lives. These spontaneous experiences, however, have even less evidential value than other spontaneous psychic experiences, for under such circumstances it is unusually difficult to decide how good an individual's memory of the event was. In fact, most of the more respectable psychical research organizations would reject out of hand any spontaneous experience reported while the subject was under the influence of drugs or alcohol.

Still, there seemed a magnificent area open for controlled research. But fate and politics intervened. The rush to psychoactive drugs during the late 1950s and early 1960s was so great that it terrified a large segment of the American population. It appeared to some that an entire generation was about to go down the drain in a drugged fantasy. There are undoubted dangers in psychoactive drugs, but the reaction was hysterical.

One of the best-publicized evangelists of the new drug gospel was Dr. Timothy Leary, who had come upon LSD through conventional research. The idea got around that not only was the casual street use of psychedelics dangerous, but even research was not to be trusted. So when the government began to crack down on the use of the drugs, it came down heavily on drug research as well by simply making it virtually impossible to legally obtain LSD and other psychedelics for any purpose.

Even without the legal difficulties, psychedelic drugs bid fair to give parapsychologists a hard time. If a century of tests has proved nothing else, it is that if ESP does indeed exist, it is an elusive ability. A tremendous amount of energy has been expended on trying to develop standardized tests which will in some way quantify this ability. But subjects under the influence of psychedelic drugs don't usually want to cooperate with standard tests.

One of the few places in the country where research with psychedelic drugs has been able to continue legally is the Maryland Psychiatric Research Center. The late Dr. Walter Pahnke, director of clinical sciences at the Center, had conducted some pilot experiments to determine what LSD did to ESP scores. The results were not encouraging. He observed that the subjects were often fearful or ill after they took the drugs and thus too preoccupied to take ESP tests. "Psychedelic drug effects can also be so novel, dramatic and interesting," he said, "that a subject may have some reluctance to attend to such a mundane task as guessing the contents of a sealed envelope."

Pahnke was still hopeful that psychedelic drugs would provide "an exciting challenge for parapsychological research in the future," but unless and until there is a change in the laws regarding the use of psychedelics for research, this door is going to remain closed.

8
HUMAN PROGRAMMING

EARLY in January of 1974 a young woman named Alice Weitzman sailed a paper airplane out of the window of her New York City apartment. The paper plane landed at the feet of a mother and child out for a walk. The mother unfolded the airplane and found that it contained a desperate note. Alice Weitzman claimed that she was being held prisoner in her apartment, and that her captors were about to move her to some other secret location. When the mother looked up, she saw the young woman waving frantically out of the window. Deciding this was no joke, she called the police. Forty minutes later they arrive at the apartment and found that the note indeed was no joke.

Miss Weitzman was being held by members of a radical left group called the National Caucus of Labor Committees, to which she belonged. Shortly before the incident took place, she had apparently begun to express some skepticism about the group's activities. The members of the group had come to believe that there was a vast conspiracy against them involving, among other organizations, the CIA, the Soviet KGB, British intelligence, the New York City police department and the Rockefeller family. They also believe, or at least say, that the future of the human race depends upon them. In a speech the leader of the group said, "The human race is at stake. Either we win or there is no humanity. That's the way she's cut."

According to *New York Times* reporter Paul L. Montgomery, the group had begun as a fairly ordinary left wing group, no different from a dozen others that existed in New York and elsewhere during the 1960s. But by the 1970s they had, step by step, drawn in upon themselves and decided, not only that their small group, perhaps three hundred in all, were the saviors of the world, but also that a vast conspiracy had been hatched against them. More sinister still, they had come to believe that some of their own members had been captured by their enemies and secretly "programmed" to kill the group's leader.

Before the explosion over Miss Weitzman, the group had already attempted to "deprogram" several members. One was sent to the hospital when he was found running through the streets screaming, "Decontrol me! Decontrol me!"

The members of the group, most of whom are young, middle-class, and apparently intelligent, are, it appears, dead serious about the idea of programming. When their activities came under scrutiny of the police, and ultimately were reported in the media, the group responded with a veritable flood of press releases about the conspiracy and "programming" and "brainwashing."

Reporter Montgomery found that "members seem incapable of talking about anything but the brainwashing and the conspiracy . . . there seems to be anxious expectation about who will be singled out as a brainwashing victim. Mr. Marcus [the group's leader] has told them that they are not responsible for their thoughts or actions because of the 'programming.'"

The beliefs of the Labor Committees could be dismissed as

a bizarre social aberration if they were alone in the belief in "programming" and "deprogramming" people. But they are not. These rather sinister words have cropped up with increasing frequency particularly since the kidnapping of Patty Hearst.

Is it possible? Has science developed methods by which the human mind can be controlled, so that an individual can be made to act like a machine and to perform whatever acts the controller wishes? Are there techniques which cause ordinary people to loose control of their own minds, so that not only their actions but their innermost thoughts are subject to control? A lot of people appear to believe that to a degree at least this is true.

The idea that sinister forces can turn people into puppets is hardly a new one. During the Middle Ages, Christians terrified one another with tales of the Assassins, the fanatic Moslem sect whose members would be sent out to kill enemies of the sect. These were suicide missions, for the killers had no hope of surviving their deed. It was believed that the sect's leader, the Old Man of the Mountain, reduced his followers to absolute submission through the use of drugs and "secret arts." Drugs almost certainly did play an important part in the life of the Assassins. The original name for the sect was Hashishin, users of hashish, but to the Assassins themselves, they were not puppets, but devout followers of their religion. Christians would regard clergy or laymen who went serenely to their deaths at the behest of superiors as saintly rather than sinister.

The key difference is whether one follows the most extreme orders voluntarily or not. But this difference is not at all easy to decide and the answer more often than not depends upon whether one agrees with what is being done.

During the witch craze of the Middle Ages thousands of

individuals confessed "voluntarily" to flying around on broomsticks, copulating with demons, and doing a lot of other things that are manifestly absurd. The confessions, however, were not really voluntary, since most were made after torture or at least under threat of torture. Voluntary to the Inquisitors meant that individuals weren't being tortured at the moment that they made the confession. Johan Weyer, an early enemy of the witchcraft persecutions, commented that "We are not all witches, because we have not all been tortured."

Yet there is something about these confessions that should give us pause. An unknown percentage of the confessions may well have been more or less accurate, because some people did engage in bizarre practices that the Church came to label as witchcraft. These practices apparently involved drug use. Thus, when the people confessed to riding out on broomsticks, and the like, they may have been confessing to drugged hallucinations that they had actually experienced.

But more significantly for our discussion here is the possibility that people who engaged in none of these practices still became convinced of their guilt. Accused as well as accusers thoroughly believed in the possibility of witchcraft and of diabolic intervention in human affairs. If persons of authority hammered at them day after day with the charge that they had committed certain acts, then it is conceivable that the weaker and more suggestible among them became convinced that they had indeed done such things. Why would God allow them to suffer so if they were not guilty? Thus they might have confessed, not merely to spare themselves further torture, but because they had come to fully share their accusers' fantasies. In a sense, one might conclude that such persons had been "programmed" to confess.

But if such "programming" actually took place, it was

extremely crude and obvious. The use of hypnotism opened the possibility of control of a more subtle and pervasive nature. The public was fascinated by the fictional figures of the evil hypnotist Svengali and his helpless subject Trilby, of the murderous somnambulist of the *Cabinet of Dr. Calagari,* and of the hypnotized automatons of a thousand lesser books and films. Few authorities on hypnosis believe that such control is really possible, but the reality of the control may not have been as important as the widespread belief that it was possible.

The next step in the development of human programming, at least its public image, came in the 1930s with the work of the Russian psychologist Ivan Pavlov. By careful training, Pavlov was able to condition laboratory animals to produce normally involuntary responses at a given signal. In his most famous experiments Pavlov was able to get dogs to salivate when a bell was rung. Previously it had been believed that dogs could salivate only when actually presented with food. Salivation was thought to be an inborn, involuntary response that could not be altered by any outside training. Pavlov proved that it could.

Pavlov's work concerned only the conditioning of certain automatic responses, like salivation. But it raised the possibility, or perhaps suspicion would be a better word, that voluntary functions could also be conditioned in a similar manner. That, for example, when a bell was rung a man would, against his will, recite a certain speech. Pavlov was a long way from even attempting this sort of conditioning. During Pavlov's time the "involuntary" responses were assumed to be entirely separate from the "voluntary" responses. But his work had a tremendous influence over Soviet psychology, and to those in the West who distrusted everything Soviet, there seemed something quite sinister about the whole process.

The worst fears about "Pavlovian" conditioning appeared to be confirmed during Stalin's notorious show trials of the 1930s. The world was treated to the spectacle of old Bolsheviks, men who presumably had been hardened by years of revolutionary activity and would have been well beyond caving in under normal threats of torture, parading into the witness box and meekly confessing to absurd and impossible crimes. These same prisoners then went off to their deaths without uttering (as far as we know) a word of criticism of those who had condemned them. Again the suspicion rose that the Soviets possessed some kind of mysterious "Pavlovian" conditioning techniques that could bend and break even the toughest wills. We still do not know what really happened during the trials, and their evil and mysterious reputation persists.

But what really set the idea of human programming solidly in the mind of the American public was the experience of the Korean War. During the war a small number of American prisoners of war confessed publicly to war crimes, and broadcast messages praising the North Koreans and Chinese and condemning their countrymen. Though such statements were not welcomed by the American public, people were willing to concede that men would "break" under torture. The really shocking part came after the war when some of these prisoners refused to come home when offered the opportunity to do so. Even with the direct physical threat removed, the Chinese still appeared to have some sort of power over their captives.

The Chinese have a term, *hsi nao,* which means "cleansing the mind." Edward Hunter, who first described the Chinese methods of indoctrinating prisoners in detail, coined the term "brainwashing" for this Chinese concept. The term was both sinister and mysterious, and it stuck.

The American military was quite naturally upset and more than a little frightened over what had happened, for it was the first time in United States history that soldiers had acted in such a way. A variety of studies of the "brainwashing technique" were launched.

It turned out that "brainwashing" was nothing particularly new or mysterious. It consisted mainly of breaking a man down through a combination of physical and mental stress and constantly hammering away at him with the ideas that the captor wished to put across. There was no resort to extreme physical torture as in the days of the Inquisition, though men were often tied, and occasionally beaten. The captors depended more on subtler methods—depriving the prisoner of sleep, not allowing him to go to the toilet, serving a uniformly monotonous diet, long periods of isolation, et cetera.

When a prisoner was thoroughly broken down by these stresses, a process of "education" began. The prisoner was freer than before, though still subjected to a strict regimen of reading and lectures. After a while the prisoner was encouraged to write or record a confession. The more cooperative he was, the more comforts and privileges he was likely to receive. And over it all hung the threat of a return to the severe conditions of being broken down. Ultimately the prisoner became more or less convinced that he was doing the right thing, that he had not confessed because he was weak, but rather because he had come to recognize past errors in his life.

The same basic techniques of coercion have been used by police throughout the world to get accused persons to confess, in army training camps to give raw recruits the proper *esprit de corps,* and even to an extent in fraternity initiations.

The new member is often degraded, harangued, and made to suffer considerable discomfort before he has become properly initiated. Of course, the Chinese and the North Koreans had no time limit and no restraints on the coercion. They could continue the process as long and as hard as they wished, but "brainwashing" represented merely a difference in degree, not any startling new discovery in control of human behavior.

But the "brainwashing" techniques were not in themselves the only reason for the behavior of some United States prisoners during the Korean War, for they were not irresistable. Most prisoners did not confess to anything or refuse to return to the United States. Investigators concluded that many of the prisoners were ill-prepared for the experience of being captured. They were draftees hastily trained for war, and did not have the proper background to resist the prison camp pressures. The Korean War was unpopular, many of the Americans fighting there didn't know why they were fighting, and many may have come to genuinely disagree with the war in the first place. In addition many of the prisoners had suffered bad experiences in the military and in their previous civilian life, and were dissatisfied with both America and the military well before they were captured.

The American military responded by stepping up its own indoctrination campaigns. The American POW experience was not repeated in the Vietnamese War, though that war was even more unpopular than the one in Korea. This change may have been in part due to better preparation by the military, but it probably had more to do with the character of the prisoners. Most of the American prisoners in Viet Nam were Air Force men, highly motivated and highly trained professionals. They were volunteers rather than draftees who were fighting because they had no choice.

Some of the prisoners were reported to be "friendly" to their captors, and a few issued anti-war statements, but the percentage was far smaller than it had been in Korea, and there were no cases in which prisoners refused to come home.

There was one genuinely scary moment during the war. The North Vietnamese occasionally released films of American prisoners, and in one of them a POW was shown shuffling and bowing and proclaiming in a mechanical voice that he was being well-treated. He looked like everyone's worst nightmare of a brainwashed prisoner. But after the prisoners were released, this man said that he had been putting on an act. He said what the North Vietnamese wanted him to say about his treatment, but by his actions he wished to show that his words were not to be believed. It was an effective performance.

From the experiences of two wars we can conclude that while brainwashing can be a terrible experience and an effective method of breaking a man's resistance, there is nothing supernatural or mysterious about it. The "secret" of brainwashing can be summed up in the bit of folk wisdom which holds that "every man has his breaking point."

Yet this has been widely misunderstood. It has been difficult for many Americans to accept that "our boys," too, are human, and that a few may have even genuinely come to feel that what they were doing was wrong. So the idea of "brainwashing" as some secret and mysterious communist technique based on sinister Oriental guile and Pavlovian conditioning has persisted.

In Richard Condon's popular novel *The Manchurian Candidate* an American prisoner is brainwashed by Pavlovian techniques, so that he is at the complete command of his communist masters. He can be trained to kill without hesitation long after he has been released from captivity. The book

HUMAN PROGRAMMING

is, of course, a work of fiction, but many people believed that it was, or could be, a description of grim reality.

By the late 1960s the word "programming," taken from computer technology, began to displace the word brainwashing as a description of this sort of mental control. The image was of human beings reduced to the state of robots, and then being fed a set of specific instructions which they were powerless to disobey once they were given the proper signal.

Oddly, the idea of people being programmed cropped up most frequently in the area of religion. The late 1960s and early 1970s saw the growth of the Jesus Movement. The Jesus Movement was a general term for a collection of groups that espoused rigid Biblical fundamentalism, and often advocated radical communal life styles. These groups held considerable appeal for many young people, and they attracted a great deal of publicity.

The more radical among these groups demanded total commitment from their members. The young converts would leave their families, sometimes never to return. If they did make a brief visit, they would often denounce their parents' lives as "godless," warn them of their eternal damnation, and answer all questions and entreaties with stock Biblical phrases.

Parents were first baffled and then horrified by this transformation that had overtaken their sons and daughters. Attempts to reason with them simply triggered the standard Biblical quotes. Threats or pleading were usually countered with sullen silence or furious denunciations. Some parents tried stronger methods. They employed force and sometimes weapons to get their children away from the religious communities, and then tried to lock them up, or in some cases actually had them committed to mental institutions. Usually the children simply waited for a chance to escape right back to the community from which they had been "rescued."

The situation was not historically unique. In other eras children abandoned the beliefs of their parents for a passionate commitment to a new and different doctrine. Then such changes were often called the work of the devil. But the devil is not quite the powerful figure today that he once was, and the transformation had to be ascribed to something else—brainwashing or programming.

A variety of rumors began to circulate. Children were being drugged, chained, hypnotized and beaten into submission by the sect. They were being conditioned to hate their parents, and serve the leaders of the sect with slavish loyalty.

Into this emotionally explosive situation stepped a man named Ted Patrick. Patrick was a former California state official who had declared a holy war against the more radical Jesus groups. He claimed that he could successfully "deprogram" the young converts. Patrick's services were engaged by a number of distraught parents. These activities kept his name in the newspapers, and occasionally got him into court. Many of those whom Patrick "deprograms" have to be physically removed from the communes or other places in which they are living—in short, they have to be kidnapped. This is always done with the consent and sometimes the assistance of the parents, but in some cases the converts have already reached legal age.

The subjects of some the kidnappings later expressed gratitude to Patrick and their parents for "saving" them, but others who have resisted deprogramming were not so forgiving. Usually even those refused to sign complaints against Patrick, either because their religious communities did not want the trouble and publicity or because they would also have had to swear out complaints against their parents. But charges have occasionally been brought against Ted Patrick.

In May 1974 he was convicted of falsely imprisoning two young women in Denver, in connection with his deprogramming efforts. A number of earlier cases had ended in Patrick's acquittal.

What does "deprogramming" consist of? Patrick is a bit vague about what goes on in a deprogramming session. In 1973, CBS News did a five-part series on his methods. Some, though not all, of the sessions of the attempted deprogramming of a twenty-year-old girl were filmed. They consisted primarily of Patrick hammering away at the young convert's beliefs for hours on end. There were also some highly emotional moments when the parents were brought in. The series made Patrick and the deprogramming look bad, and he must have realized this, for at one point he ordered the cameramen out entirely. Many viewers probably reacted with delight when they heard that the girl, after being successfully "deprogrammed," grabbed the first opportunity she could to run away and return to the group from which she had been taken.

During the TV series civil liberties lawyers were interviewed, and they insisted that Patrick's methods were illegal, since the girl was of legal age and being held against her will. Yet police authorities were unwilling to intervene, even while she was being carried off, protesting loudly right before their eyes and right in front of television cameramen.

There is no evidence of any physical coercion in the deprogramming, that is, aside from the basic fact that a person is being held against his or her will. The parents of the girl in the CBS series seemed to think of deprogramming in terms of an exorcism. They spoke of demons being expelled from their daughter's body. In the Denver, Colorado, case two young women said Patrick accused them of being "zombies" and "possessed by the devil." Patrick claims great success for his method, but there are no hard figures, and it certainly failed to work with CBS cameramen around.

In order to be "deprogrammed," a subject must first, of course, be "programmed." Is there any activity that goes on within these groups that could lend itself to such a description?

The question is not easy to answer. Members of the Jesus groups deny that they place any unusual pressures on new converts. The change, they say, is brought about "by the direct action of God." However, a report on the most radical of these groups, The Children of God, issued by the Attorney General of the State of New York lists the alleged involuntary imprisonment of a woman and her child at one Texas commune, and the statements of several ex-members who said they had to make their escape from the communes by "devious means" such as sneaking away at night or feigning illness that required hospitalization or a doctor's care.

My own personal observation of one of New York State's larger Children of God colonies (a name the group prefers to commune) makes it difficult for me to believe that any sort of prison camp, brainwashing program could possibly have been undertaken there. The physical setting was simply too open. There were no guards, fences, or even very many locks. Anyone who wished to "escape" would merely have had to walk less than a mile to the town and into the office of the local police department. The police, who were extremely hostile to the sect, would surely have given any escapee full protection.

On several visits to the colony headquarters I was allowed to go anywhere I wished. While I may have missed a hidden room in which people were kept chained, I sincerely doubt it. I also observed the preparation of a couple of meals at the urging of colony leaders, who wished to prove that no drugs were being put in the food. In retrospect the whole idea seems silly, but the charge of drugging food had been made and was believed in some quarters. The local attitude toward the group was very negative at the time, and they finally moved away, whether because of pressure or because of a policy of wandering, which is part of The Children of God philosophy, one could not be sure.

Members told me how local law enforcement officials and parents had invaded the colony at gunpoint looking for members who had been "kidnapped." Others told of being forcibly spirited away and locked up or put in mental institutions by their parents. In one case I was able to confirm the story by talking to the member's mother.

The only reasonable conclusion one could draw is that far more physical coercion has been exercised against members of The Children of God, and presumably against similar sects, than by them. Local law enforcement officials also seem willing to withhold normal protection from members of such groups.

Where then do these tales of chaining and drugging come from? There is a strong tendency on our part to think the worst of the religious nonconformist, and the history of unorthodox religion in America is filled with similar tales that circulated about the early Mormons, Shakers, Jehovah's Witnesses and even the Methodists.

However, physical coercion is not the only element involved in winning converts and influencing the innocent. New members are subjected to heavy psychological pressure, some of it reminiscent of prison camp experiences. The new members of The Children of God—babes, as they are called —are almost completely dependent upon the group elders. The elders make all the decisions that affect the babes' lives —when they are to get up, what they are to eat, and where they will go. And members are constantly on the go, being shifted from one colony to another and often from one country to another. The Nazis would shift their prisoners from one camp to another, this being an effective method of breaking their will.

For the first few weeks new recruits are never on their own. I was told that an older member even accompanied them when they went to the toilet, though I did not observe this. There are endless Bible readings and constant repetition of certain favorite Biblical phrases. Some quotes are painted on large signs and hung in bedrooms.

Many of those who join a group like The Children of God join at a moment of personal crisis. Most of those that I talked to told of hideous experiences with drugs, prostitution, jail and an overpowering sense of loneliness and worthlessness. Just when they felt that they were "at the bottom," the stories ran, they were "saved" by the group. One might say that life itself had already broken them down, and they were open to "brainwashing."

Yet stories like these, like the testimonies of reformed drunks and saved sinners at a skid row mission meeting, tend to be suspect. But I did have an opportunity to interview a young man who had just that morning wandered into the colony looking for help. He did indeed appear to be in a bad way. He seemed unable to talk coherently, and he broke down and cried several times during our interview.

The picture can be made to sound pretty grim and sinister. But the colony that I visited didn't give that impression at all. On the contrary, there appeared to be a genuine sense of warmth and community among the members. Nor did the individuals behave like the wind-up robots of the brainwashing nightmare.

Responses to questions were generally rather standard appeals to Biblical quotation. In fact, most of the colony members didn't know very much about the Bible outside of the selected quotes. In addition, I got the distinct impression that people were on their best behavior—that they were hiding the really radical nature of their doctrine in an attempt to appear more respectable.

But what young and vigorous religious group has ever encouraged free discussion among its members? The whole notion of authority and direction in both one's physical and mental life is part of the great appeal of such groups. For people who have felt lost and purposeless it is often a great relief that someone will tell them when to get up and what to do, even what to think. There is no need to confront difficult questions about life, if they appear to be answered by a few simple Bible quotes. This perhaps is not a way of life which is attractive to most of us, but we need not resort to explanations involving drugs and strange powers of suggestion to explain its appeal. Indeed, this sort of fantasying simply adds to the mystique of such groups, and in a way probably makes them more appealing than they otherwise would be, for it imparts a slightly supernatural air.

One might well question the morality of taking an individual at a moment of crisis, then repeating the same phrases over and over again to him until he uncritically accepts the doctrine or runs away. But this is just exactly the technique used by early revivalists, and indeed still is used today in some churches. Charles Grandison Finney, the father of modern revivalism and the man who codified the techniques now employed so successfully by Billy Graham and others, said that a person had to be "broken down before the Lord" before he could truly be converted. The "breaking down" process might take the form of a long series of physically and mentally exhausting meetings wherein the hearers were harangued with terrifying descriptions of what would happen to them through all eternity if they did not convert immediately. And Finney's methods were comparatively gentle. Some of his more flamboyant predecessors were accused of driving people to insanity and suicide during their campaigns. They were also occasionally accused of practicing "mesmerism" or even of "bewitching" people.

Some of the Jesus groups, incidentally, are not averse to turning the charges of brainwashing and hypnotism against their enemies. When the followers of Guru Maharaj Ji held a big festival in the Houston Astrodome late in 1973, one of the most memorable sights was that of Jesus group demonstrators screaming at those entering the Astrodome that they were going to be hypnotized if they went inside.

The followers of the Guru Maharaj Ji's Divine Light Mission and members of other Eastern religious sects like Hare Krishna regard "the mind," that is, rational thought, as an obstruction to reaching satori, or whatever it is that they hold as the aim of life. There is nothing unique about this. Many now respectable Christian groups regard rational thought as inferior and often antagonistic to faith. In order to resolve doubts, one is often encouraged to pray rather than think.

Still some see Guru Maharaj Ji's techniques as infinitely more malevolent. Journalist Ken Kelley, who studied the Divine Light Mission, has written: "Guru Maharaj Ji instills in his followers a mind-control device that would surely make the Central Intelligence Agency envious. Called 'The Knowledge,' it is a combination of several ancient yoga meditation techniques that members must practice several times a day, and particularly when the mind threatens to reassert its rational thrust. So when the Guru's ostensible message of peace and love is overshadowed by the violent

HUMAN PROGRAMMING

practice that can accompany it, a follower can purge the mind of all contradictions by meditating them into oblivion." So meditation, at least in one view, can serve as a "mind control device." But for how long? The movement led by Guru Maharaj Ji is only a few years old, and its growth in the United States has been fantastic. But signs of strain are showing up in the Divine Light Mission and the Guru Maharaj Ji may soon go the way of many other now forgotten gurus and masters who were to transform the world, only to be swallowed up by it.

More serious for society at large is yet another aspect of programming or brainwashing. This is euphemistically called "behavior modification" and it is used, though no one seems sure how extensively, in the United States prison system.

This practice got into the news early in 1974 when the federal government bowed to pressure that had been building up against the behavior modification programs that it was funding. The most controversial of these was known as START—an acronym for Special Treatment And Rehabilitative Treatment. The project being tested at the federal prison in Springfield, Missouri, involved trying to alter the behavior of "troublesome" inmates by first locking them in cells for hours and depriving them of all privileges, then rewarding them if they behaved properly by restoring their privileges. If the prisoners had been American POWs, the same treatment would be called brainwashing.

The project had become an object of extreme hatred and fear to prison inmates. Some threatened hunger strikes and even suicide if the START program were instituted. It was denounced as "Pavlovian" and "Clockwork Orange," a reference to a popular movie about the future in which an attempt is made to alter a prisoner's behavior by various conditioning methods.

Along with canceling START, the federal government also banned the use of federal anticrime money for behavior modification programs anywhere. But this does not mean that behavior modification attempts have been stopped in prisons and elsewhere; they haven't, and there appears to be no accurate information on how many of these programs exist, how they work, or what the results are. Some of the programs reportedly involve the use of drugs that make the subjects sick, and of electric shocks.

Outside of prison some similar programs are voluntary. An individual who is trying to cure himself of a bad habit, such as excessive drinking or smoking, can be given a drug that will make him violently ill every time he takes a drink or smokes a cigarette.

Persons convicted of child molesting have, at their own request, been treated with painful electric shocks. The purpose is to condition their sexual impulses away from children. A few pilot drug addiction programs employ similar conditioning techniques.

The American Psychological Association, the nation's main organization of psychologists, however, believes that behavior modification is not only effective, but a lot more humane than methods used in the past. They contended that a banning of all behavior modification techniques "will result in a regression to outmoded, unsystematic forms of inhumanity in prisons that have characterized society's past treatment of its criminal offenders."

The Association's statement continued, "Behavior modification involves a large number of procedures, some of which are clearly abhorrent to psychologists as well as to the public. Other procedures, however, are humane, benign, systematic, educational and effective."

HUMAN PROGRAMMING

Few, even among severe critics of behavior modification techniques, advocate a complete ban on it. They think that it is at least possible that some type of treatment can be beneficial. What they contend is that the programs must be monitored far more carefully than they have in the past and that they should be voluntary.

So some attempts at behavior modifications will probably be with us for a long time to come. But how effective are modern techniques of behavior modification?

Cutting through all the hysteria and mystification that has surrounded the subject of "brainwashing," "programming" or "behavior modification," one can conclude that while it is possible to significantly alter the behavior of another person, such alteration is not easy, nor have the techniques progressed significantly since the days of the Inquisition. But what of the future?

So far we have discussed primarily means of changing behavior from the outside. But today, we can get inside the brain in two important ways: drugs and surgery.

Psychoactive drugs have gotten a great deal of publicity over the last twenty years, and such drugs have been used in attempts at controlling behavior. During the Stalin era sodium Pentothal, the "truth serum," was used extensively on political prisoners. The Nazis were reported to have used barbiturates on prisoners, assuming that they would somehow "weaken the will." Neither drug proved particularly successful.

In the early 1960s there was a good deal of talk about the use of psychochemicals in warfare, and the United States Army was actively engaged in experimenting with chemical agents for altering behavior. One army promotional film showed how a chemical could be used to make a cat flee in terror when a mouse was released into its cage. There was speculation about a "fear gas" that could be released on a battlefield and cause the enemy to drop their weapons and run. There was also speculative talk of chemicals that could be released into the water supply of an enemy city. The chemicals would make the entire population passive and unwilling to fight. This idea, incidentally, was picked up by some of those who opposed fluoridation of water supplies. They said it was part of a communist plot to destroy America's will to resist. There have also been occasional threats, probably not serious, to put LSD in a city's water supply.

Opponents of army chemical warfare claimed that all the talk of nonlethal gas was nothing more than a cover for experiments with extremely lethal nerve gas. Gas, as a weapon of war, has had a very bad reputation since World War I, and extensive experimentation with lethal gases was not looked upon with favor by the American public.

Just how far the Army got with its psychochemical experiments was, and still is, a secret. But there have been no press releases extolling the virtues of "nonlethal" gas for over ten years now. The entire chemical warfare research program of the Army has been severely curtailed, and to all outward indications there is no military psychochemical program at the present time. It is a fairly good bet that if there ever was much research in nonlethal psychochemicals, nothing very startling was discovered. The only nonlethal gas still in wide use is teargas or similar agents, which all have powerful physical rather than psychological effects.

A whole pharmacopeia of psychoactive drugs, most notably LSD, burst upon the American scene during the 1960s. In the first flush of enthusiasm it was claimed that the drugs could do anything from curing alcoholism to putting an individual in direct touch with God. They could produce dramatic, and sometimes long-term alterations in human behavior. But the drugs proved to be highly unstable, that is, one could never be sure just what sort of a behavior alteration would result. They were not the sort of substances that appeared promising agents for controlling the behavior of others.

Whereas in the late 1950s and early 1960s we were treated to pictures of cats driven to terror by the use of chemicals, by the late 1960s there was a new image—monkeys or other animals with strange devices sticking out of their skulls, whose emotional states could be controlled by radio signals.

This is a technique known as electrical stimulation of the brain, or ESB. The process is not new; it was discovered in the 1930s by a Swiss psychologist named Walter Rudolf Hess. Hess found that by implanting tiny electrodes in a particular part of a cat's brain, and then sending a weak electrical current through the electrodes, the cat would exhibit all the overt signs of extreme fear. The electrodes and the electrical stimulation itself was painless, and different types of behavior could be altered by placing the electrodes in different areas of the brain.

We know that brain activity is in part electrical. What brain researchers assume is that the electrical stimulation actually mimics the natural neural signals, and sets off the response. ESB therefore gives scientists a way interfering very directly and very basically with brain activity.

Since the 1930s research in ESB has progressed steadily if unspectacularly. Scientists have been able to refine their techniques and map the brain more accurately to find out which areas control which type of behavior. In 1967, Dr. Jose M. R. Delgado, a Yale neurophysiologist and one of the country's leading researchers in ESB, arranged a highly dramatic demonstration. Dr. Delgado himself, complete with red cape, stood in the middle of an arena with a charging bull bearing down upon him. The bull had an electrode implanted in its brain, and concealed beneath Dr. Delgado's red cape was a portable radio transmitter. By the flick of a switch Dr. Delgado stopped the charging animal dead in its tracks.

This demonstration made the front page of *The New York Times* and sent a shiver down a lot of people's spines. If an animal can be so easily controlled, could the same be done to a human being? The answer is yes, of course; there is no basic difference between the physical brain of a cat or bull and the brain of a human being. During brain surgery electrical probes have been applied to various areas of the brain and have elicited responses in much the same way as they are obtained from experimental animals. So ESB can work in the human brain. The next question is—has it already been used?

A man named Peter Mason thinks that it has. In January, 1972, Mason picketed the offices of the *Washington Post* wearing a sandwich board that said "FREE MY BRAIN." Mason claimed that his actions and thoughts were being controlled by a device placed within his body when he was six years old.

Mason told *Post* reporter Tom Huth that he had filed suit in United States district court to force the United States government "to stop manipulating my body."

Peter Mason is not alone in the belief that he is being controlled by a device implanted within his body. Stories of this type are surprisingly, even alarmingly, common. When I worked as a science editor, I received letters from dozens of different individuals who had essentially the same story to tell—their actions, even their thoughts, were being manipulated, either by some sort of unknown rays or by a device implanted within their bodies usually after an operation.

One man used to circularize magazine editors with a regular mimeographed newsletter that arrived every two or three months. It contained a detailed and poignant description of all the terrible things that he thought were happening to him because of this control. Over the three years in which I received this particular circular, I read how the man lost job after job, quarreled with friends and relatives, was evicted from his apartment—all, of course, because he was being manipulated from within. Finally the circulars just stopped coming. I have no idea what happened. Unlike Peter Mason, this particular individual did not seem entirely sure of who was controlling him or why.

Others tended to blame the CIA, the communists, the Catholic Church or beings from outer space for their troubles. Another commonly expressed belief is that others—husband, wife, neighbors—were being controlled electronically and were compelled to perform hostile acts.

Psychiatrists are naturally well aware of delusions of this nature. The belief that oneself or others are being controlled by an outside force is hardly a new one. In past ages it was the Devil or evil magicians or hypnotists who were doing the controlling. Today it is often a vague but powerful force called "the government" or even "the space people" that control by means of implanted electrical devices.

Currently, though, the Devil seems to be making something of a comeback as an object of fear. The immediate reason is the book *The Exorcist* and the tremendously popular movie made from it. More basically, polls show that there has been a growing belief in the reality of the Devil over the last decade. As a result a lot of people feel that they are being controlled or possessed.

The Reverend Richard Woods, a Dominican at Loyola University in Chicago who wrote a book on the Devil, said recently: "I've received dozens of calls from people who are horribly frightened or so confused that they have begun to lose their grip on reality. I also know of two kids who came out of the movie thinking that they were possessed and they have now been hospitalized." Other priests have reported similar experiences.

But diabolical possession and exorcism may well be a passing fad. The real deep fear is still that of the electrical device in the brain.

Could these fantasies become reality in the near future? Probably not, for ESB, though it seems quite powerful, is at present a very blunt instrument. Gross emotional states like fear can be induced by electrical stimulation. But more subtle controls like "lift the right arm" or "close your eyes" are not only beyond the state of our technology, they are beyond our theory as well. We have only the faintest notion of how this kind of voluntary response is carried within the brain, and no idea at all as to how it could be interfered with.

The concept of implanting thoughts, ideas or information within the brain is even farther out. The brain has often been compared to a master computer, and science fiction regularly deals with situations where data is fed to the human brain in much the same way it is to a computer. But the analogy between brain and computer is one of limited usefulness. We know how memory is stored within a computer; we do not know how the brain stores memory. We know the process by which a computer acts on data and arrives at a conclusion. We do not know how a thought moves through the brain. There are theories aplenty, but they are of only the most general sort. The brain may someday yield its innermost secrets to research, but scientists who have worked in the field do not think that this day will come soon.

Two other areas of possible control should be mentioned here. The first is direct chemical stimulation of the brain. Some researchers have found that by adding certain chemicals directly to particular areas of the brain, states like fear or hunger can be stimulated more effectively than with ESB. Brain activity is both electrical and chemical, and the chemical appears to be more amenable to outside interference. But chemical stimulation, too, is still an extremely blunt instrument, and when dealing with the possibility of behavior control, its drawbacks are obvious. It involves applying chemicals directly to the brain through a hole in the skull. This could be done only under rigid laboratory conditions.

The second area of concern is psychosurgery. This is the destruction, by surgery, of specific portions of the brain. Again the idea is not new. In the 1930s and 1940s a radical form of psychosurgery called lobotomy was performed on severely disturbed individuals. The aim of the surgery was to correct violently anti-social behavior, to calm hopelessly agitated individuals, and to release the severely depressed from their crippling emotions. The surgery, though, resulted in such massive personality changes within the patient that society reacted to it with a kind of collective horror. Lobotomy, it was said, turned people into human vegetables or modern-day zombies. It became regarded as a "fate worse than death."

The practice, virtually abandoned for years, has resurfaced under the name of psychosurgery. Today improved surgical techniques make a more delicate brain operation possible. Psychosurgery, say its supporters, is still a drastic procedure, but it is preferable to a lifetime of hopeless institutionalization either in a mental institution or prison. It holds out the promise of returning the patient or prisoner to at least a semblance of a normal life.

But since psychosurgery has been performed on, or suggested for, mental patients and prisoners, two groups that have severely limited abilities to choose whether or not they would really wish such an operation, the subject has raised a host of legal and ethical as well as medical questions. It is at best a controversial technique of limited usefulness. As a method by which a Manchurian Candidate form of behavior control could be exercised, it faces the same limitations as ESB and chemical stimulation of the brain. Keen as the surgeon's knife may be, it is still a blunt instrument in the delicate human brain.

The last few years have seen enormous progress in laboratory study of behavior control. Like atomic energy, this area of research is one that is not without its grave potential hazards. Perhaps someday mankind may well wish that it had never embarked upon research in the field of behavior control in the first place. But that day is not yet at hand. This is one time when we should probably be grateful for the slow pace of scientific progress.

9
THE SCIENCE OF RELIGIOUS EXPERIENCE

ALONG with about two hundred other people I had come to the gymnasium for a prayer meeting. The meeting began with some singing to guitar accompaniment. After the singing, we all sat quietly for a few moments. Then sort of a gentle murmur started up in the group.

The young man next to me was talking, apparently to himself, but not in English or any other intelligible language. This was speaking in tongues, or glossolalia. Perhaps half the group was engaged in the same thing. After a while there was silence, then someone was "moved" to get up and read a selection from the Bible. There was some more singing and a bit of banging on tambourines. A couple of people related what they had "learned" or "felt" during the week since the last meeting. There was more quiet speaking in tongues.

This went on for an hour, and all the while an air of tension and expectancy built in the room. Something more was supposed to happen. After about an hour and a quarter a woman who had been sitting with her eyes closed and her arms raised over her head began speaking in a loud voice. The words were English, but the meaning obscure. What was clear was that it was supposed to be the voice of God or Jesus speaking directly through her as a medium. The enigmatic key phrase to the prophecy was "participate in the architecture of my Church." All over the room paper and pens were produced as people wrote down the words.

A short time later another woman, also apparently entranced, issued another prophecy. It was a rather bland and general appeal for Christians to join together. Again there was much note-taking.

The emotional high point of the evening came when the young man next to me burst out chanting in tongues. It was very regular and rhythmical and sounded like a Latin chant to someone who knows no Latin. When he was finished, someone shouted, "Oh, Lord, grant us an interpretation of your words."

Psychologists insist that glossolalia is not an "unknown language" at all, but rather a series of meaningless sounds. Certain individuals have a tendency to utter such sounds during periods of emotional intensity. Moreover, say psychologists, glossolalia behavior is infectious—when one person starts, others with similar tendencies will take it up. The behavior is learned, the more one engages in glossolalia, the better one becomes at it, and the more easily one is able to start speaking in tongues. Many religious people, however, consider such explanations totally inadequate. Even if the sounds are not really a language, the experience of glossolalia, they say, is a deeply religious one.

The meeting ended, apparently by general consent, after about two hours. Everyone in the group seemed, if not exhausted, at least pleasantly relaxed. After the meeting about thirty people retired to the chapel for a healing ceremony that involved laying on of hands, some praying in tongues and a good deal of joyful laughing.

THE SCIENCE OF RELIGIOUS EXPERIENCE

The meeting was by no means rowdy or even very emotional. Camp meeting revivalists would have considered it dead and dry, and members of some of the more emotional fundamentalist churches would have concluded that the Holy Spirit was not really operating within the group.

What was surprising was that this particular meeting was held in the gymnasium of a Roman Catholic seminary. Most of the participants were practicing Catholics, and among them were at least one priest and several nuns. Some Protestants and a few Jews also attended the meeting. Ten years ago gatherings of this sort for "receiving the Holy Spirit" would have been utterly unthinkable among regular Catholics.

Practically everyone in and out of the Church agrees that the Roman Catholic Church in America (and perhaps worldwide) is in serious trouble. Church attendance is down, priests and nuns are leaving at an unprecedented rate, and recruitment in religious orders is way down. Catholic schools are closing so rapidly that there is a genuine fear that the entire system is on the verge of collapse.

The one segment of the Church that is showing vigorous growth is represented by the meeting we have described. It is called the Charismatic Renewal or Catholic Pentecostal movement, and has attracted hundreds of thousands of adherents over the last few years. The attitude of the Church hierarchy toward this movement is one of cautious tolerance, though the emotionalism of the charismatic meetings genuinely upsets many more traditional Catholics, and the reliance on direct illumination of the worshiper by God would seem to present some thorny theological problems. The charismatic movement is a genuine grass-roots phenomenon, and although many Catholics simply do not know what to make of it the movement is clearly filling a deeply felt need.

Pentecostalism is the belief that the "gifts" the New Testament describes as having been given to the early Christians on Pentecost, especially glossolalia and faith healing, were neither allegorical nor restricted to the early Church, but are still in effect as signs of the power of the Holy Spirit. Charisma, a word that has had a vogue in politics, in this context means the spiritual power that is given to an individual. Modern Pentecostalism was confined to Protestant fundamentalist groups until just a few years ago. Even today Catholics often prefer to call themselves Charismatics rather than Pentecostals.

They insist there is nothing new about what they are doing, rather that they are rediscovering something vital about the Church that has been lost sight of for centuries. To emphasize this they usually refer to the Charismatic *Renewal* Movement.

The Catholics are not alone. The charismatic movement has also grown vigorously among the Episcopalians and other nonfundamentalist Protestant denominations. Many formerly sedate Protestant ministers are taking a new interest in the more emotional Pentecostal services. All of this comes in the face of a decline in membership among most main-line Protestant churches, whereas "fringe" churches, including many of the Holiness and Pentecostal churches, have either held their membership or actually increased it.

Much of the appeal of the Jesus Movement among young people comes from encouraging intense religious experience. The currently fashionable Eastern religions, like that of the Guru Maharaj Ji and Hare Krishna, also place direct experience rather than theology or ritual at the center of their religion. The persistence, indeed the growth of the deeply mystical and fervent Hasidic movement among Jews, is an indication that the same feelings are found in Jewish culture as well. Professor John B. Snook, in his book *Going Further:*

THE SCIENCE OF RELIGIOUS EXPERIENCE

Life-and-Death Religion in America, concludes that many of the new and vigorous religious movements in America are "experience-oriented."

"In other words," he writes, "much of the current interest in religion is highly personal among many young people who are totally uninterested in familiar religious traditions except as they furnish ideas for meditation and individual guidance, and occasionally for visionary communal efforts."

Though many religious leaders would probably disagree, one could make the case that much of what is most lively and vital in religion in America today is an outgrowth of the recent fascination with psychoactive drugs. The belief that modern life is both too material and over-intellectualized, and that it ignores more meaningful inner realities, was one of the basic dogmas of the drug counterculture. This belief also counts heavily in the appeal of many modern religious movements. A large percentage of the young involved in today's religious movements trace their initial interest in religion to experimenting with drugs. And the meaning of slogans like "turn on to Jesus" is obvious enough.

Of course, the desire for intense religious experience is neither particularly new nor uniquely American. It has been an important part of most religions throughout history. What is perhaps a little surprising is that in America, where ten years ago religion appeared to be getting more "rational," "intellectual" and "social," in short more of this world, the deeply committed religious movements of the last few years have been those centered on intensely personal, emotional religious experiences. Doubly surprising, perhaps, because this type of religion has had a special appeal to the well-educated, relatively affluent young.

Religious experience is clearly a deep, deeply desired and highly significant part of the lives of many persons even in our highly technological society.

It has been argued that religious experience is something that has helped to shape human consciousness throughout history, and we are simply rediscovering that fact.

No matter what the age or culture in which these experiences occur, one can find similarities. Over two hundred and fifty years ago a young Oxford graduate, troubled by religious doubts, attended a religious meeting at which the subject was "the change which God works in the heart through faith in Christ." This young man was highly intelligent, well-educated and had grown up at a time when religious skepticism was prevalent, particularly among the educated. Yet at this meeting he wrote later, "I felt my heart strangely warmed. I felt I did trust in Christ, Christ alone, for salvation; and an assurance was given me, that He had taken away my sins, even mine, and saved me from the law of sin and death."

The young man's name was John Wesley, and the year was 1738. Writes Professor Snook, "The language may not be exactly what you would find today, but it isn't really that different either. The important thing is that it follows an old pattern..." The experience was not only central to Wesley's life, but as it turned out, the experience was significant for an enormous number of other people, for Wesley went on to found the Methodist Church.

Religious experience, though it is basically intensely personal, does tend to fall into certain patterns. One could almost chart the progress of the conversion experience as described by Wesley.

We have already mentioned how the study of ESP and other psychic or paranormal phenomena was inspired in large measure by religious feelings. It is, therefore, rather strange that the subject of religious experience itself has

THE SCIENCE OF RELIGIOUS EXPERIENCE 189

rarely been made the object of any sort of regular psychic investigation. Certainly accounts of religious experiences are as numerous and as reliable as accounts of ghosts, poltergeists, apparitions or even spontaneous telepathic experiences. As far as the effect they may have on an individual's life, they are infinitely more important.

At the turn of the century the great American psychologist, philosopher and supporter of psychical research, William James, was invited to give a series of lectures on religion at the University of Edinburgh. The lectures created a mild sensation. It was James's contention that all theology, all religious philosophy, were secondary, even absurd. Yet he also believed that religion itself may have been "mankind's most important function." How could this be? The core of religion, said James, was the religious experience itself. The way in which any individual interpreted the experience, that is, the particular creed to which one adhered, was quite unimportant.

To bolster his contention, James cited a huge variety of evidence from history, from the biographies of religious men and women, and from accounts collected personally or by fellow psychologists and psychical researchers. The accounts he cited ranged from the chilling descriptions of the practices of ascetic medieval saints who arranged ingenious tortures for themselves so that they could subdue the flesh and better know God's will, to the rather simple statements of ordinary people who felt the presence of "something greater" than themselves which helped to sustain them in times of trouble.

James saw that religious feelings and experiences not only brought about spiritual or internal changes within an individual, but often transformed his or her outward life, sometimes in a most extraordinary and dramatic way.

William James drew few hard-and-fast conclusions from

the mass of evidence which he examined except to say, "The whole drift of my education goes to persuade me that the world of our present consciousness is only one out of many worlds of consciousness that exist, and that those other worlds must contain experiences which have a meaning for our life also; and that although in the main their experiences and those of this world keep discrete, yet the two become continuous at certain points, and higher energies filter in."

James suggested that there might be some sort of a science of religion, based on a study of religious experience rather than on theology or history of religion. The aim would have been to study those "certain points" at which the ordinary world and the world of other consciousness met and "higher energies filter in." James's lectures, though rather radical for the orthodox Christian audience before which they were delivered, were nonetheless well-received. They were collected and edited into a book entitled *The Varieties of Religious Experience,* first published in 1902 and still widely sold to this day. And yet practically nothing was done about his suggestion of developing a "science of religion."

Since one is not dealing with physical religious experiences, that is, the reputed levitations of saints, healing, and the like, there is no place for physical science in such a study. These experiences are entirely internal, and fall into the realm of psychology. Psychologists, however, tended to view religious experiences, particularly the more novel and exotic ones, as some form of pathology. For their part most religious people tended to resent the intrusion of science into their internal lives. They felt that science was not at all sympathetic to their point of view, and that it would only mock or defile what was to them central in life. It is almost an axiom to the religious that a spiritual experience is beyond measurement and beyond description. But the business of

THE SCIENCE OF RELIGIOUS EXPERIENCE 191

science is measurement and description.

As a result, except where it touched upon more familiar forms of psychical research, there was no organized attempt to study religious experiences as such until recently.

The unlikely pioneer in this controversial field is a seventy-eight-year-old British marine biologist, Sir Alister Hardy. Sir Alister is acutely aware that because of his age there are many who regard his search as a sentimental whim of a senile old man—"Poor old Hardy, I can imagine them saying."

Sir Alister, however, is no stranger to controversy and throughout his long career has shown a willingness to champion ideas others might consider unorthodox or even crazy. In addition to his lifelong work in marine biology, he has also had a long-standing interest in psychical research, and is past president of the British Society for Psychical Research. For a prominent scientist to so openly display interest in the fringes of science is to invite ridicule from one's colleagues, and Sir Alister has received his share.

Not only that, back in the 1960s Sir Alister advanced the highly unorthodox hypothesis that *Homo sapiens* evolved, not from an aggressive ground-living carnivorous ape, but rather from an ape that spent much of its time in the water and lived a pacific, cooperative existence. Sir Alister's ideas were adopted by feminists and given wide public attention in a book called *The Descent of Woman* by Ellen Morgan, published in 1973.

Sir Alister's decision to study religious experience in man was not a hasty one made late in life. He had always been interested in religion, and had been aiming at this sort of study for at least a quarter of a century. Finally he got his wish.

Sir Alister directs the Religious Experience Research Unit (RERU) which operates primarily out of a converted candy shop in a sixteenth-century building in Holywell, Oxford, England. The buildings are owned by Manchester College and leased to the RERU.

Peter Lewis, writing in the British publication *Observer,* said, "The very name has a strange utopian ring about it. It calls up a picture of monks strapped into electrodes in some transcendental laboratory." In fact, the Unit, which operates with a tiny staff and on a limited budget, is more like a polling operation at this stage of its existence.

"Science cannot analyze the essence of religious experience any more than it can analyze poetry or human love," says Sir Alister. Well, then, what is the RERU doing?

"Our main aim is to build up a body of knowledge about religious experience in the present-day world which we hope will demonstrate whether or not it does in fact form, as I believe, an important part of man's makeup: something which may perhaps be psychologically as fundamental as sex, but much less understood. From a detailed study of thousands of examples we hope in time to learn much more about the nature of this experience. And finally . . . we hope it may lead to an experimental approach to religion." One reporter characterized the work as a "Kinsey Report" on religion, a description which Sir Alister emphatically rejects.

The first step in this process, not yet completed, is the collection of a mass of reports of religious experiences. Sir Alister compares the work of the RERU with that of the early naturalists who went about the world collecting and classifying specimens of plants and animals. "My conviction," says Sir Alister, "has always been that ecology, the study of the interrelationships of organisms, will be applied to human life. All my life I have sampled the sea, building up an ecological picture of a hidden world which I could not examine at first hand, even with an aqualung. In a way I am now casting my nets into a different kind of ocean." This is the ocean of human spiritual experience.

How does one decide whether an experience is "religious" or not, and how can such experiences be collected? Sir Alister's first step was to contact all the regular religious journals in Great Britain and ask them to print appeals for accounts of experiences that their readers considered religious. The results of this attempt were disappointing. While some thirty religious journals actually printed the appeal, there were a mere two hundred responses, and a disconcertingly high percentage of these came from elderly ladies.

So Sir Alister decided to cast his nets more widely. He contacted several publications such as the *Times* and *Observer,* which had a more general readership, and made an appeal over the BBC. This resulted in several thousand responses, most encouraging, but still the researchers feared that they were tapping only a limited stratum of British society. The The next step was to get their message into the *Mail,* a mass-circulation publication with a less intellectual appeal. The Unit has also circulated its own appeal. The aim of all of this is to collect some 5,000 records (testimonies, the religious might call them) of experiences that might be defined as religious.

Such sampling methods would, of course, cause George Gallup and Lewis Harris to throw up their hands in despair. Accounts collected by appeal do not give an accurate sampling of the religious experience of the population as a whole. They are drawn only from those individuals who read particular publications, and are interested enough, and willing to write letters. The classic example of the dangers of this type of sampling came in 1932 when *Liberty* Magazine printed a sample presidental ballot. On the basis of the returns of that ballot *Liberty* confidently predicted that Herbert Hoover would defeat Franklin Roosevelt.

A more scientifically selected polling of religious or mystical experiences has already been made in the United States by the Opinion Research Center of the University of Chicago. The Center conducted in-depth interviews with a sampling of 1500 persons in the United States. From its sample the Center says the results can be projected onto 175 million adults in the United States who are not in college, the armed forces, hospitals or prisons.

According to Father Andrew Greeley, a Catholic priest and sociologist who works at the Center, "Thirty-six percent of Americans interviewed say they have at some time in their lives felt as though they were close to a powerful force that seemed to lift them out of themselves."

"A mystical experience," explained Father Greeley, "is one of being at peace with everything and everyone and of having genuine knowledge of being in personal touch with ultimate reality.

"A person who has it is religious whether he goes to church or not, whether he professes any doctrine or not—simply because he claims to have seen and to know the way things really are."

Most commonly, said Father Greeley, the experience was brief and took place under comparatively ordinary circumstances. "It usually lasted less than an hour, and often only a few minutes. Some said they felt it while watching a sunset, others while staring into a log fire."

Father Greeley was quick to point out that none of these experiences were reported to be drug-induced. "Instead, we found they [the people interviewed for the survey] had backgrounds of warm family relationships. Our findings are far from the popular picture of mystically inclined people as repressed, unhappy or guilt-ridden.

"Our samples showed that Protestants are almost twice as likely as Catholics to have such experiences, and Irish-Americans are more likely to have them than any other ethnic group. Black people also seem highly receptive to mystical experiences."

Beyond the mystical experiences the survey found an even greater number of people reported other strange experiences. Some 61 percent had feelings of *déjà vu*—the sensation of having been somewhere or done something before, when one has not. Thirty-four percent of those contacted said that they had experienced some form of communication with the dead.

Father Greeley said that *déjà vu* experiences, ESP, and contact with the dead, when reported by subjects, were not counted among mystical experiences, although they are what might be called paranormal or supranormal.

"We found that young people are more likely to experience *déjà vu* than old people. Young and old seem more likely to experience ESP than the middle-aged. And contact with the dead is most frequent among those in their 40s and 50s."

Back in 1889 the British Society for Psychical Research conducted what they called the "Census of Hallucinations." The census question was, "Have you ever, when believing yourself to be completely awake, had a vivid impression of seeing or being touched by a living being or inanimate object or of hearing a voice; which impression, so far as you could discover, was not due to any external physical cause?"

The SPR sample was not scientifically selected. SPR members essentially just contacted their friends, but still the census did reach some 17,000 persons. The result was that approximately 10 percent of those asked reported having such an experience. Fifty-eight years after the original survey, Dr. D. J. West asked the same question of a more carefully chosen sample. This time 14 percent reported such an experience.

Experiences "beyond the normal," and often considerably beyond, are a good deal more common, or perhaps "normal," than one might suspect.

The RERU is not at this point trying to determine the frequency of religious experiences, but rather is trying to get an idea of the sort of experience or feeling that people classify as religious. The accounts they receive are broken down, and the elements within them classified. These are some of the elements that are found in accounts received by the RERU to date:

>Sensory or quasi-sensory experiences
>Behavioral experiences
>Cognitive experiences
>Affective experiences
>Impressions of "Providence"
>Dynamic patterns in experience
>Dream experiences
>Trance experiences
>Drug experiences

These main elements are then subdivided. For example, in the sensory or quasi-sensory experiences are separated into those involving visual, auditory, touch and on rare occasions smell experiences. There are further subdivisions. Under the heading of visual might be found those who (a) see "visions," (b) experience some extraordinary illumination, (c) see a light, (d) feel a unity with their surroundings and/or with other people, (e) have out-of-the-body experiences, (f) have *déjà vu* experiences, and (g) have an impression of a heightened appearance of their surroundings. Auditory and touch experiences are similarly subdivided.

Affective experiences can be subdivided into such classifications as sense of security, assurance and peace; awe; wonder; reverence; exaltation; ecstasy; excitement; sense of integration, freedom and wholeness, all the way to such things as feelings of fear and horror and indifference and detachment.

Any religious experience may contain characteristics from several different subheadings. The resulting classification looks something like the letters and numbers used in chemical formulas like H_2O. Chemical formulas tell the chemist at a glance the nature and composition of the compound. The formula for religious experiences might appear as A6b or B1a, 4am7a.

The task of classifying thousands of accounts of varying length and quality is, as should be quite obvious, an exceedingly difficult one and of necessity highly subjective. But Sir Alister feels there is nothing "unscientific" about such a system. He compares what his group is doing with the work of the early biologists, who set about trying to classify previously unknown zoological or biological specimens. Much of early biology was concerned with taxonomy, or classification of specimens. Today problems of classification consume very little of the biologist's time, but establishing a clear system was a necessary first step in the development of modern biology.

The next step is to try to draw some sort of meaningful order out of the classification—to find out, for example, whether certain ages, sexes or upbringings are more prone to certain types of experiences.

Follow-up work on the original accounts has already begun. Some of the respondents have been asked to restate their original experiences in terms of a specially drawn set of questions so that they can be more closely compared and contrasted.

Farther down the road is the polling of a representative sample of the population of Britain, just as the Opinion Research Center has polled a sample of the United States public. This sample would be interviewed in depth, and each individual would be given examples like those sent to the RERU and asked whether they have ever experienced similar feelings. From such a sample the RERU hopes to get an idea of how widespread these experiences are, and how much they may vary in different segments of the population. This ambitious undertaking still lies in the future because of limited funds. The Opinion Research Center project employed the services of several hundred interviewers and the use of computers. Currently Sir Alister doesn't even have a secretary and answers all his letters by hand.

Sir Alister realizes that he will probably not live to see his project beyond the "natural history" phase, that is, the collection and classification of material. He continually warns those interested in his work against jumping to hasty conclusions on the basis of inadequate data. "It is a long term research and must have secure foundations; it cannot be hurried."

What sort of experiences come into the office of the RERU? There are, of course, what Sir Alister calls the "Z category"—communications from the lunatic fringe. Some of these accounts were actually written from inside of mental institutions. But he says, "The percentage of these apparently unbalanced writings is much smaller than I had expected; they are all being carefully filed, for who can be sure that they may not contain elements worth studying, and at least they may provide valuable material for the psychiatrists. Some in the Z are not really experiences at all, but

THE SCIENCE OF RELIGIOUS EXPERIENCE

letters sermonizing on the writer's religious views."

Most of the experiences received so far might be called fairly mild ones, not the intense and overpowering experiences so often described in biographies of saints and other religious figures. Feelings of exaltation, ecstasy and excitement come far down on the list of affective experiences received by the researchers. It is these more ordinary experiences in which the RERU is most interested at present, for they are most certainly the most widespread, and ultimately may have the most to reveal about the essence of religious experience in general.

Typical are letters from people who, without warning, claim to have experienced nothing more than a sudden "feeling" or "presence" that changed their whole outlook. Owing to the fact that all accounts sent to the RERU are kept in strict confidence, published sections can give no clue as to who the writer might be, but here are some examples from the files:

"One day," reports a correspondent, "as I was walking along Marylebone Road I was suddenly seized with an extraordinary sense of great joy and exaltation, as though a marvelous beam of spiritual power had shot through me, linking me in rapture with the world, the universe, Life with a capital L, and all the beings around me. All delight and power, all things living, all time fused in a brief second."

"I heard nothing," says another, "yet it was as if I were *surrounded* by *golden light,* and as if I only had to reach out my hand to touch God himself who was so surrounding to me with his compassion." The feeling of a unity with all nature is a common feature of many reported experiences.

"It seemed to me that, in some way, I was extending into my surroundings and was becoming one with them," revealed one writer. "At the same time I felt a sense of lightness, exhilaration and power as if I was beginning to understand the true meaning of the whole Universe."

Even more specific on the sense of unity is the note that says, "It is difficult to describe, but in some way because of this feeling I feel united to all people, to all living things. Of recent years the feeling has become so strong that I am now training to become a social worker because I find that I must help people; in some way I feel their unhappiness as my own."

Reports another writer: "When I was on holiday, aged 17, I watched an ant striving to drag a bit of twig through a patch of sun on a brick wall in the graveyard of a Greek church, while chanting came from within the white building. The feeling aroused in me was quite unanticipated, welling up from great depth, and essentially timeless. The concentration of simplicity and innocence was intensely of some vital present. I've had similar experiences on buses, suddenly watching people and being aware how right everything essentially is."

Many of the accounts strike the outside observer as almost literary in tone, that is, they seemed inspired or heavily colored by the type of religious and inspirational writing which abounds in church circles. How honest or valid are the accounts? Sir Alister admits that some are undoubtedly exaggerated. Still he insists, "No one with an unbiased mind, I believe, can read the majority of these accounts without being impressed by a feeling of their deep sincerity. Our stressing the confidential treatment of the material has I am sure been an important factor. I am convinced that the vast majority of these are indeed sincere and important human documents."

In addition to the collection and classification of accounts of religious experiences, the RERU also engages in some more orthodox types of parapsychology experiments. Though this is not the main thrust of the research, Sir Alister does not shy away from the possible connection between ESP and religion. "If the scientific world can be convinced that thought patterns can be transferred from one mind to another by other than physical means it lends plausibility to the possibility of individuals making contact with something outside of the self, something transcendental."

What is this something? "I am not saying what this is. I have no metaphysical ideas. I think it is a waste of time to postulate them at present. But whatever it is, it does have a marked effect upon people's behavior."

There is little doubt that Sir Alister Hardy and his co-workers have a religious bias. They know how they want their research to come out. In early 1974, Sir Alister was at work on a book developed from a series of lectures he had given some years earlier. He made a point that the book was to be put out by the same publisher that issued the best-selling volume *The Naked Ape,* by Desmond Morris. This book presented man as an animal controlled by behavior patterns inherited from his primate ancestors. Sir Alister says that his book will be a study of "man the religious animal," and that it will serve as something of a rejoinder to the Morris view.

It is hardly a secret that one of the aims of the RERU is to destroy the idea that all living organisms are simply physiochemical machines that have evolved by chance.

Does this frankly religious outlook disqualify Sir Alister and persons similarly disposed from any scientific study of religion? Would it be impossible for anyone with such an outlook to approach the subject with "cool scientific objectivity"? Well, perhaps, but in fact "cool scientific objectivity" is something of a myth. Very few scientists will start a line of research without having a pretty strong idea as to how they think the experiments will come out, and a strong sense of how they hope they will come out. Scientists can, and have, become passionately attached to theories that they are trying to prove. This does not necessarily destroy the value of their work.

Disputes flare up all the time within the scientific community, and the debates are often conducted with anything but "cool scientific objectivity." In general, the only people who are "objective" about a subject are those who don't know anything about it or don't care. The problem is not that a researcher has a point of view, or a bias, but that he does not allow his bias to make him ignore or distort available experimental evidence. There are times when the evidence for one side or the other becomes so overwhelming that even an honest partisan can no longer ignore it, and has to change his views.

Sir Alister doesn't think that his religious outlook is a dogmatic one; on the contrary, he thinks that many of his more orthodox scientific critics are the dogmatic ones. "The chief scientific dogma of our time is that everything that is scientific can ultimately be reduced to terms of physics and chemistry," he says. "I am a Darwinian. I am a believer in the DNA genetic code. I believe that every physical action of the body can be described in physiochemical terms. But I am a heretic to this extent: I think it is likely that mental events, while linked to the physical system, belong to a different order of nature."

Sir Alister feels sure that the majority of his scientific colleagues are wrong in regarding mental events as irrelevant, and believing that they can ultimately be reduced to simple stimulus-response behavior.

The purely physiochemical view fails to hold up when

THE SCIENCE OF RELIGIOUS EXPERIENCE 203

confronted with the problem of consciousness, he says. "To many scientists consciousness indeed prompts an embarrassing question. We have no right to assume that the higher animals, at least, are not conscious beings. Can anyone who has kept and become fond of a dog, a cat or a horse believe that they are unconscious organic machines? Can we really believe that consciousness is but . . . a by-product of an entirely physiochemical brain? It is the fundamental nature of this consciousness that we do not understand. In the field of consciousness as we experience it lie all our feelings of purpose, love, joy, sorrow, with the sense of the sacred, the sense of right and wrong, the appreciation of beauty, indeed all of the things that really matter in life."

Sir Alister's biological training has led him to conclude that consciousness has also had a part to play in evolution. "I believe conscious behavior is another selective force, alongside the environment and predators and the higher you go in the animal world, the greater the part it plays within the system, leading eventually to tool-making, speech and to modern man. So to my mind the Darwinian doctrine is not in the higher realms anything like the materialist doctrine it is assumed to be.

"Having restored consciousness to the scheme of things— and it took me 25 years of thinking and reading before I could really accept this [doctrine] as a Darwinian"—Sir Alister contends that the mind-body relationship is a genuine mystery, not an illusion as more materialistically oriented scientists contend. "We just don't understand the mind-body relationship and we have no idea how to account for consciousness. Consciousness has to be taken as a fundamental datum. I think that mental events belong to a different order of nature which is related in a mysterious way with events in the brain. Is it not rather impertinent to assume we have already explored the whole of the universe? There may be a whole realm of nature in which mental events take place connected with the physical side, through the nervous systems of living things. In the end there will probably be a reconciliation into one system. But at present it is indefensible to insist on Monism [the philosophical system which holds that there is only one basic substance or principle as the ground of reality] by disregarding half the evidence."

Alister Hardy is by no means the first person to have raised such questions about a possible difference between the physical and the mental and/or spiritual world. They have been discussed in one form or another since the beginning of the scientific revolution in the seventeenth century. Today, with all of the interest in "altered states of consciousness" and "other realities," the questions are as pressing for many people as they ever were.

The work of the RERU is not going to solve basic questions like the nature of the universe or the nature of man. But what the Unit does hope to accomplish is to throw additional light on "the spiritual side of man." "If we build up our knowledge," says Sir Alister, "natural theology could be as exciting and vital as molecular biology is today."

"Natural theology" based on scientific truth should lead to an experimental kind of religion. This would not necessarily be experimental in the laboratory sense of the word. Rather Sir Alister hopes that people will be able to test this sort of religion to see if it works for them. "Religion cannot have any force if it is entirely based on traditions and documents from the past."

Sir Alister hopes that people who were skeptical of religion on materialistic grounds might be willing to experiment with religion as a method of reaching the power that seems to flow from religious experience. He doesn't believe that religion can bring about any alteration in physical events. One is not going to get rich or gain personal safety. What might one conceivably obtain from this "natural religion"? "Some measure of spiritual strength and guidance for a better way of life or how best to deal with some difficulty or achieve some worthwhile purpose." These are the sort of benefits that people most often say that they have obtained from their religious experiences. It is a modest aim, when compared to the miracle cures or instant riches and power sometimes attributed to a religious experience. But surely a feeling of support and guidance is something that we all yearn for at times, and a way of finding it is an immensely worthwhile goal.

Sir Alister has gathered some impressive support for his admittedly unorthodox undertaking. Writing in the publication *New Scientist,* one of Britain's leading scientific journals, John Wren-Lewis, an industrial scientist, says the real importance of Sir Alister's study is that it takes the concept of religious experience seriously and treats it as a central feature of human life. The mere existence of such an investigation may have great value for society, Wren-Lewis believes: "The only effective way of counteracting the growing feeling among the young that science is opposed to personal values is to demonstrate in practice the spirit of openness which is the real essence of science."

Even more enthusiastic support comes from the Rev. Joseph McCulloch: "No field of research could be more relevant to the deepest need of 20th-century man, the need which lies behind, beyond and within all his present problems."

Surely the need, or at least the desire, for religious experience is still very much with us in this last third of the twentieth century. The writer Martin Gardner has observed that the current revival of emotional religious fundamentalism among the young has taken practically everybody by surprise.

"The liberal churches are now half-filled on Sunday mornings mostly with sad-faced elders who are there largely from habit. They sing tuneless hymns with vacuous phrases. They recite dreary creeds they no longer believe. They drink a communion wine that has lost even its symbolic savor. On the other side of town, Pentecostal churches are jammed with bright-eyed youngsters who are belting out the old melodious songs about the Cross, shouting 'Thank you, Jesus!' and having a marvelous time."

Whether the tiny RERU, with its gentle, almost quaint approach to religious experience, is going to succeed in shedding any real light on "man as a religious animal" only time will tell. But at the very least Sir Alister Hardy and his colleagues recognized the importance of the subject before it became fashionable to do so. And for that reason, if no other, their work deserves serious attention.

SELECTED BIBLIOGRAPHY

Barber, Theodore Xenophon, et al. *Biofeedback and Self-Control.* Chicago: Aldine-Atherton, 1971.
Calder, Nigel. *The Mind of Man.* New York: Viking, 1970.
Darnton, Robert. *Mesmerism.* New York: Schocken, 1970.
Dauven, Jean. *The Powers of Hypnosis.* New York: Stein and Day, 1969.
Delgado, José M. R. *Physical Control of the Mind.* New York: Harper and Row, 1969.
De Ropp, Robert. *The Master Game,* New York: Delacorte, 1968.
Desmond, Shaw. *The Power of Faith Healing.* New York: Liveright, 1957.
Ebon, Martin (editor). *Psychic Discoveries by the Russians.* New York: New American Library, 1971.
_____. *Prophecy in Our Time.* New York: New American Library, 1968.
Edmunds, Simeon. *Hypnotism and ESP.* Los Angeles: Wilshire Book Co., 1967.
Estabrooks, G. H. *Hypnotism.* New York: Dutton, 1957.
Foulkes, David. *The Psychology of Sleep.* New York: Scribner's, 1966.
Gauld, Alan. *The Founders of Psychical Research.* New York: Schocken, 1968.
Green, Celia. *Out-of-the-Body Experiences.* New York: Ballantine, 1972.
Greenhouse, Herbert B. *Premonitions: A Leap into the Future.* New York: Bernard Geis, 1972.
Gustaitis, Rasa. *Turning On.* New York: Macmillan, 1969.
Hardy, Sir Alister. *The Living Stream.* London: Collins, 1965.

SELECTED BIBLIOGRAPHY

Hebb, D. O. *The Organization of Behavior.* New York: Wiley, 1949.
Heenan, Edward F. (editor). *Mystery, Magic and Miracle.* Englewood Cliffs, N. J.: Prentice-Hall, 1973.
Hembree, Charles R. *Fruits of the Spirit.* Grand Rapids, Mich.: Baker Book House, 1969.
Hyde, Margaret O., Marks, Edward, and Wells, James B. *Mysteries of the Mind.* New York: McGraw-Hill, 1972.
James, William. *The Varieties of Religious Experience.* New York: Crowell-Collier, 1961.
———. *The Will to Believe.* New York: Dover, 1956.
Jonas, Gerald. *Visceral Learning.* New York: Viking, 1973.
Karlins, Marvin, and Andrews, Lewis M. *Biofeedback—Turning on the Power of Your Mind.* Philadelphia: Lippincott, 1972.
Koestler, Arthur. *The Roots of Coincidence: An Excursion into Parapsychology.* New York: Random House, 1972.
Lawrence, Jodi. *Alpha Brain Waves.* New York: Avon, 1972.
Lilly, John C. *The Center of the Cyclone.* New York: Julian Press, 1972.
Luce, G., and Segal, J. *Sleep.* New York: Coward-McCann, 1966.
Masters, R. E. L., and Houston, Jean. *The Varieties of Psychedelic Experience.* New York: Holt, Rinehart and Winston, 1966.
McCreery, Charles. *Psychical Phenomena and the Physical World.* New York: Ballantine, 1973.
Myers, F. W. H. *Human Personality and Its Survival of Bodily Death.* London: Longmans, Green, 1954.
Ostrander, Sheila, and Schroeder, Lynn. *Psychic Discoveries Behind the Iron Curtain.* Englewood Cliffs, N.J.: Prentice-Hall, 1972.
Pearce, Joseph Chilton. *The Crack in the Cosmic Egg.* New York: Julian, 1972.
Podmore, Frank. *From Mesmer to Christian Science.* New Hyde Park, N.Y.: University Books, 1963.
———. *Mediums of the Nineteenth Century* (2 vols). New Hyde Park, N.Y.: University Books, 1963.
Ranaghan, Kevin, and Ranaghan, Dorothy. *Catholic Pentecostals.* Paramus, N.J.: Paulist Press, 1969.
Rose, Louis. *Faith Healing.* Middlesex, England: Penguin, 1971.
Rosenfeld, Edward. *The Book of Highs.* New York: Quadrangle, 1973.
Ryzl, Milan. *Parapsychology; A Scientific Approach.* New York: Hawthorne, 1970.
Skinner, B. F. *Beyond Freedom and Dignity.* New York: Knopf, 1971.

SELECTED BIBLIOGRAPHY

Smith, Susy. *The Enigma of Out-of-Body Travel.* New York: Garrett Publications, 1965.
———. *ESP and Hypnosis.* New York: Macmillan, 1973.
Snook, John B. *Going Further: Life-and-Death Religion in America.* Englewood Cliffs, N.J.: Prentice-Hall, 1973.
Spraggett, Allen. *The Unexplained.* New York: New American Library, 1967.
Tart, Charles T. (editor). *Altered States of Consciousness.* New York: Wiley, 1969.
Tompkins, Peter, and Bird, Christopher. *The Secret Life of Plants.* New York: Harper, 1973.
Tyrrell, G. N. M. *Apparitions* (revised). London: Gerald Duckworth, 1953.
Ullman, Montague, Krippner, Stanley, and Vaughan, Alan. *Dream Telepathy.* New York: Macmillan, 1973.
Underhill, Evelyn. *Mysticism.* New York: Dutton, 1961.
Van Over, Raymond. *Unfinished Man.* New York: World, 1972.
Watson, Lyall. *Supernature.* New York: Doubleday, 1973.
West, D. J. *Psychical Research Today.* London: Gerald Duckworth, 1954.
Wilson, Colin. *The Occult: A History.* New York: Random House, 1971.

INDEX

Age regression, 144–147, 154
Alcoholics Anonymous, 30
Aldrin, Edwin "Buzz," 2
All-India Institute of Medical Science, 18–19, 44
Altered States of Consciousness Induction Device, 151
American Association for the Advancement of Science, 4–5
American Psychological Association, 27, 174
Anad, Bal K., 44
Armstrong, Neil, 2
Assassins, 158
Astral projection, 134
Astronauts, 1–6, 15

Backster, Cleve, 126–129
Bagchi, Basu K., 18, 43
Barber, Theodore X., 40
Beatles, 17, 22
"Bedside manner," physician's, 71
Beecher, Henry, 73–74
Behavior modification, 173–175
Bellows, George, 102
Benson, Herbert, 24–26
Berger, Hans, 10–11
Bernhardt, Sarah, 42

Bernstein, Morey, 145
Bessent, Malcolm, 104–105, 109, 110–111, 114
Beuno, St., 67, 81, 83
Biofeedback, 10, 14, 27, 32, 33, 35, 38–39, 46–52
Bioplasma, 121, 123
Bird, Christopher, 128–129
Blackburn, Douglas, 141
Book of Highs, The (Rosenfeld), 137, 148
Brain
 chemical stimulation of the, 180–181
 electrical stimulation of the, 177–180
"Brainwashing," 161–165, 166, 170, 172, 173, 175
Brain waves, 10–20, 32, 33, 34, 38, 100, 143
Brosse, Therese, 42
Bureau des Constatations Medicales, 79–81

Cabinet of Dr. Calagari, 160
Campbell, Colin, 23
Cancer, 68–71, 75–76
Carrel, Alexis, 79
Catholic Church, 185–186

INDEX

Catholic Pentecostal movement, 185–186
Cayce, Edgar, 66–67
Center of the Cyclone, The (Lilly), 149
Charismatic Renewal movement, 185–186
Charles II, King (England), 56
Chemical stimulation of the brain, 180–181
Children of God, 168–171
Christianity, 55
Christian Science, 61–64, 67
Church of Scientology, 63–64
Church of the Sacred Alpha, 10
Clairvoyance, 153
"Clockwork Orange," 173
Coleridge, Samuel Taylor, 90
Columbus, Christopher, 2
Conditioning, 51, 52, 160–161, 164, 174
Condon, Richard, 164
Consciousness, 7, 8, 9, 21, 39, 42, 203
  altered states of, 137–155
  of plants, 126–131
Conway, 140–141
Corkell, Mrs. Anthony, 146
Creativity tests, 33–34
"Cure by biopsy," 75
"Cybertronic Detector," 32

Davidson, Richard, 108
Déjà vu experiences, 195, 196
Delgado, Jose M. R., 177–178
Deprogramming, 166–168
Descent of Woman, The (Morgan), 191
Devil, 179
Dewan, Edmund, 15
Divine Light Mission, 172–173
Dreams, 13, 87–116
Drugs, 16–17, 26, 138, 153–155, 158, 159, 174, 175, 176–177, 187

Eddy, Mary Baker, 61–63, 140
Edwards, Harry, 65–66, 81
Electrical stimulation of the brain, 177–180
Electrocardiogram (EKG), 43, 47
Electroencephalograph (EEG), 10–15, 18, 19, 20, 24, 32, 42, 91, 143

Electromyograph (EMG), 49–50
Elizabeth I, Queen (England), 56
Engel, Bernard, 46, 47
Estebany, Osker, 84–86
Evans, Frederick J., 73
Exorcist, The, 179
Exotic psychic phenomena, 117–136
Extrasensory perception (ESP), 3–5, 11, 79, 87–116, 120, 143, 151–152, 154, 155, 188, 195

Faith, 48, 53
Faith healing, 53–86, 186
Farrow, Mia, 22
Feedback, *see* Biofeedback
Feedback Church of America, 38
Ferrer, St. Vincent, 56
"Fight Flight syndrome," 25
Finney, Charles Grandison, 171–172
Flournoy, T., 144
Foulkes, David, 112
Foundation for Mind Research, 107, 151
Franklin, Benjamin, 60
Freud, Sigmund, 69–70, 90, 94
From India to the Planet Mars (Flournoy), 145
Fromm, Erich, 93

Galen, 72
Galston, Arthur W., 130
Gardner, Martin, 205
Glossolalia, 183–184, 186
Goldfinger, Steve, 103
Grad, Bernard, 84
Graham, Billy, 171
Grateful Dead, The, 104, 114
Greatrakes, Valentine, 57
Greeley, Andrew, 194–195
Green, Alyce, 19
Green, Elmer, 19, 51
Gurney, Edmund, 140, 141

Hallucinations, 148, 159, 195
Hardy, Sir Alister, 191–206
Hare Kirshna, 172, 186
Hashishin, 158
Hasidic movement, 186

Healing, faith, 53–86, 186
Healing Waters, 64
Hearst, Patty, 158
Hermon, Harry, 151
Hess, Walter Rudolf, 177
Hirai, Tomio, 20, 21
Hohenlohe, Prince Alexander von, 57–58, 60
Holy Feedback Church, 10
Honorton, Charles, 151–152
Houdini, Harry, 42
Houston, Jean, 106–107, 151
Hubbard, L. Ron, 63–64
Hughes, Mrs. Charles, 95
Human programming, 156–182
Hunter, Edward, 161
Huth, Tom, 178
Hypnotism, 31, 35, 61, 74, 139–147, 160, 172

Intelligence, 33–34
International Meditation Society, 24

Jacob, Zouave, 58–59
James, William, 153, 189–190
Jesus Movement, 165–172, 186
Ji, Maharaj, 172–173, 186
Johnson, Douglas, 108
Jones, Christopher, 38

Kamiya, Joe, 13–16, 34, 38
Kasamatsu, Akira, 20, 21
Kayak disease, 137
Kekulé, Friedrich, 90
Kelley, Ken, 172
Kennedy, John F., 96, 103
Kiefer, Durand, 38
Kirlian, Mr. and Mrs. Semyon, 119
Kirlian photography, 119–125
'Knowledge, The,' 172
Koestler, Arthur, 7
Korean War, 161–163
Krippner, Stanley, 88, 104, 106, 108, 109–110, 111
Kuhlman, Kathryn, 65

Leary, Timothy, 154
Lewis, Peter, 192

Lilly, John C., 149–150
Lincoln, Abraham, 97
Linden, William, 34
Lobotomy, 181
Lourdes, shrine at, 79–81
LSD, 16–17, 150, 154, 155, 176

McCreery, Charles, 132
McCulloch, Joseph, 205
Magnetism, 59–61
  animal, 59, 60
Maharishi International University, 25
Maimonides Medical Center (Brooklyn), 88, 99–116, 150–151
Manchurian Candidate, The (Condon), 164
Mantra, 23, 28, 29, 39
Marcus, Mr., 157
Maryland Psychiatric Research Center, 155
Mason, Peter, 178, 179
Masters, R. E. L., 106–107, 151
Mead, Margaret, 4–5
Meditation, 10, 17–39, 172–173
  transcendental, 17, 21–29
  Zen, 20–21, 38
"Meditation effect," 31
Mesmer, Franz, 59–61, 139
Mesmerism, 60–61
Middleton, J. Cannon, 95–96
"Mind control" courses, 35
Mitchell, Edgar D., 3–6, 117, 137
Monism, 204
Montgomery, Paul L., 157
Morgan, Ellen, 191
Morris, Desmond, 201
Moss, Thelma, 123
Muldoon, Sylvan, 135
Murphy, Bridey, 145–146
Myers, F. W., 6

Naked Ape, The (Morris), 201
National Aeronautics and Space Administration, 1–2
National Caucus of Labor Committees, 156–157
National Institute of Mental Health, 88
Nervous system, 41–42, 45

INDEX

autonomic, 41, 45, 48
Niebuhr, Reinhold, 33
Noetics, 5, 117

Ogilvie, Sir Heneage, 71
Opinion Research Center, 194, 198
Ornstein, Robert, 39
Osmont, Anne, 134
Ostrander, Sheila, 123, 147
Otis, Leon S., 28–29
Out-of-the-body experiences, 131–136, 150, 196

Pahnke, Walter, 155
Paracelsus, 122
Parapsychological Association, 4
Parapsychology, 5–7, 88, 115, 117, 118, 144
Parise, Felicia, 103, 104–105, 114
Patrick, Ted, 166–168
Pavlov, Ivan, 160
Pentecostalism, 185–186
Peper, Eric, 17
Photography
  Kirlian, 119–125
  spirit, 125
Pike, James A., 6–7
Placebo effect, 30–31, 33, 72–75
Plants, consciousness of, 126–131
Podmore, Frank, 140
Precognition, 108–111, 153
Programming, human, 156–182
Psychical Phenomena and the Physical World (McCreery), 132
Psychical research, 4–7, 113, 117, 120, 139
Psychic Discoveries Behind the Iron Curtain (Ostrander and Schroeder), 123, 147
Psychic forces, 8
Psychoanalysis, 70
Psychochemicals, 175–176
Psychosurgery, 181–182
Puysegur, Marquis de, 139

Quimby, Phineas Parkhurst, 61

Raikov, Vladimir L., 147

Rama, Swami, 19
Reality, 7
Reincarnation, 144
  artificial, 147
Religious experience, science of, 183–208
Religious Experience Research Unit, 191–206
Rhine, J. B., 6, 88, 153
Roberts, Oral, 64–65
Roots of Coincidence, The (Koestler), 7
Rose, Louis, 81–84
Rosenfeld, Edward, 137
Ryzl, Milan, 143

Satori, 38, 39
Schroeder, Lynn, 123, 147
Schwartz, Gary, 29, 33–34
Science and Health (Eddy), 61, 62, 63
Scientology, 63–64
Secret Life of Plants, The (Tompkins and Bird), 128
Sensory deprivation, 148–152
Simmons, Ruth, 145–146
Skinner, B. F., 51–52
Sleep research, 13, 139
Smith, George Albert, 140–141
Smith, Hélène, 145, 146
Snook, John B., 63, 186–187, 188
Snow, C. P., 118
Society for Psychical Research, 80, 82, 96, 115, 116, 140, 141, 191, 195
Soubirous, Bernadette, 79
Special Treatment and Rehabilitative Treatment (START), 173–174
Spirit photography, 125
Spiritualism, 140
Spontaneous remission, 68–69
Stalin, Joseph, 161
Stanford Research Institute, 28
Startle reaction, 19, 21
Stepanek, Pavel, 143–144
Stevenson, Ian, 94–95
Suggestion, 74–75
Susan, 108
Svengali, 160
SYNANON, 30

INDEX

Tamayo, 102
Tart, Charles T., 135–136
Taub, Edward, 27, 31
Telepathy, 100, 104, 107, 108, 111, 112, 139, 153
Titanic, 95–96, 103
Tompkins, Peter, 128–129
Trilby, 160

Ullman, Montague, 88, 104, 106, 108, 111

Van Gogh, Vincent, 102, 109, 110, 114
Varieties of Religious Experience (James), 190
Vietnamese War, 163–164
"Visceral learning," 48–49
Vogel, Marcel, 129

Wallace, Robert K., 24–26, 31
Weiss, Theodore, 46, 47
Weitzman, Alice, 156–157
Wenger, Marion A., 18, 43
Wesley, John, 188
West, D. J., 70, 80–81, 115, 195
Weyer, Johan, 159
Whatmore, George B., 50
William III, King (England), 56
Winefride, 67
Winquist, W. T., 26
Witches, 158–159
"Witches' cradle," 148, 151, 152
Woods, Richard, 179
Wren-Lewis, John, 205

Yoga
  Hatha (physical), 18, 42, 45
  Raja (meditative), 18
Yogi, Maharishi Mahesh, 17, 21–23, 33, 39
Yogis, 17–23, 40–46, 48, 50
"Yogi sleep," 19